ISBN 978-1-330-67266-2
PIBN 10090429

1 MONTH OF
FREE
READING

at
www.ForgottenBooks.com

By purchasing this book you are eligible for one month membership to ForgottenBooks.com, giving you unlimited access to our entire collection of over 700,000 titles via our web site and mobile apps.

To claim your free month visit:

www.forgottenbooks.com/free90429

SOCIAL TEACHINGS OF THE CHRISTIAN YEAR

LECTURES DELIVERED AT THE CAMBRIDGE CONFERENCE, 1918

BY

VIDA D. SCUDDER

AUTHOR OF "THE CHURCH AND THE HOUR:
REFLECTIONS OF A SOCIALIST CHURCHWOMAN," ETC.

NEW YORK
E. P. DUTTON & COMPANY
681 FIFTH AVENUE

PREFACE

People who are indifferent to organized religion are strongly advised by the author to keep away from this book. They would find it either annoying or meaningless; at best, time spent on it would be wasted, and wasted time is a serious matter in a world where no one can read what he should.

The book is written for those who care deeply and lovingly for the Christian Church; more specifically, for those in the habit of following the Seasons of the Church Year through the Anglican Prayer-Book. More specifically still it will make its strongest appeal to persons who are awake to the social gospel on which so much salutary stress is now laid, and who want to find a harmony between the precious traditions of spiritual experience and the new life astir in our hearts, impelling us to a strange and untried world.

Christians of a liberal turn of mind and an affection for the Prayer-Book! This may seem a restricted group, but it is larger than some people think. Moreover, so far as the author is concerned, the embargo on reading is off in the case

438998

of any persons religiously disposed. Her chief ambition will be realized, should the book quicken social passion and faith in devout minds.

Three strong convictions have inspired the writing.

The first is, that a new world-order is surely on the way. To affix labels would be premature and impertinent; but, on broad lines, what is happening is already evident. Democracy is reaching out from the political to the industrial sphere; the old class-alignments are doomed to vanish; large types of wealth and large sections of industry are to be socialized; and our children are destined to live in a civilization as different from that of our fathers as that was different from mediæval Europe. To speak more technically, a system based mainly on private capital and the incentive of private profit, is in process of yielding to a system partly at least based on some form of socialized capital, and on incentive of another kind.

The second conviction is, that the tremendous changes in prospect can only be safely accomplished if religion supplies them with a soul. A socialist and atheistic world is conceivable; but every Christian knows that it would carry its doom within it. Such a world would be a travesty of our dearest hopes. In the noble words of the

Lambeth Committee Report on International Relations (1920), ''A social order for which humanity hungers is beyond the reach of merely human expedients. Nothing will establish peace on the earth but a new creation from God in response to repentance and prayer.''

The third conviction is, that the ancient faith of the Cross is competent to inspire this new creation; that the principles which must guide the coming change are all implicit in the cycle of Christian truths; and that these truths urgently need to be restudied, for the light they throw on social thought and duty in these difficult times.

The subject of this book is, then, the social inferences to be drawn from the Mysteries of the Christian faith as expressed in the sacramental system of the Church. But these Mysteries are studied, not from the point of view of formal theology, but rather from that of Christian experience. It is a book for very simple people, not conversant with the discussions of the schools, but trained by Mother Church in love, and faith, and will, through her patient reiteration during the changing seasons from Advent to Trinity, of what she holds most essential and most dear.

Even while the book has been on the typewriter, a change has been passing over the spirit of the Churches. Twenty years ago, they were hesitant and conservative; signs of sympathy with the forces, even then rising, of industrial democracy were few and far between. Christian radicals, never lacking at any moment of religious history, were generally regarded askance, and were certainly not in official favor. All but insensibly, the situation has altered. Today, courageous expressions of scarcely veiled agreement with advanced social views multiply from month to month. Reference need only be made to the stirring Statement of four Roman Catholic Bishops; to the fine "Social Creed of the Churches," issued by the Federal Council which represents United Protestantism in America; to the Report of the Archbishop's Fifth Committee of Enquiry in England; and to the epoch-making Lambeth Reports. Christianity, in Anglo-Saxon countries at least, is placing itself formally and officially, under our eyes, on the side of the New Order

But Statements, Resolutions, and Reports are useless except as a beginning. The coming change involves a new Christian ethic, in the development of which every member of Christ's Church should share; and the formation of this ethic, in turn, demands a re-examination of the Christian formulæ from the new point of view.

This book, approaching its subject from a special direction, aims to bring out a neglected aspect of the Mind of the Church. Needless to say, it does not therefore discount or discredit the importance of the personal aspect habitually emphasized. In studying the social implications of Christian experience and Christian doctrine, it seeks to supplement the older understanding of the faith by drawing new wealth from an exhaustless store.

Adelynroad, South Byfield, Mass.
Holy Cross Day
September 14, 1920.

TABLE OF CONTENTS

xi

Table of Contents

SOCIAL TEACHINGS OF THE CHRISTIAN YEAR

"In Divinity I keep the road, and though not in an implicite yet in an humble faith, follow the great Wheele of the Church by which I move."

—Sir Thomas Browne, *Religio Medici.*

SOCIAL TEACHINGS
OF THE
CHRISTIAN YEAR

INTRODUCTION

THE slow formation of a Christian social mind is one of the greatest things happening in this great epoch; for it means that Christian people are regaining a passionate allegiance to the Master's purpose, the creation of the Kingdom of iGod on earth. They are eager and ready to follow this purpose, no matter how revolutionary be the changes in the political or economic order to which it may lead.

The enquiry as to what the purpose involves is no easy one; it calls for all the sanity, courage and intellectual acumen that the seeker can command. "Speak, Lord, for Thy servant heareth," must be the cry of the soul; but to distinguish the Lord's words in the din of conflicting theories is a grave and difficult matter. The Christian turns to the

Church of Christ for guidance, and he does not turn in vain. Only, he must realize that the authentic voice of the Church reaches him, not through any casual or temporary channel, but through the spiritual truths on which she concentrates the hearts of her children. To Church folk, at least, the solemn recurrent rhythms of the Sacred Seasons reveal ever new depths of meaning in the mysteries of Judgment and Incarnation, of Penitence, Atonement and Resurrection, in the thought of the Church as the tabernacle of the Indwelling Spirit, and in that consummation of Catholic faith, the doctrine of the Holy Trinity. Every one of these mysteries carries a distinct social message; taken together, they are for the Christian the ultimate source of all true social theory and the guide to all right social action.

This is not a statement that will commend itself widely. Dogma is unfashionable, and the Church Year is saturated with dogma. Modern radicals, appalled by the failure of Christianity to control the behavior of classes or nations, turn from its doctrines with contempt. If they are religiously disposed, they point to the Sermon on the Mount, and summon us sharply away from the formulæ of the Church to the words of the Master. Christian ethic, rather than the Christian creed, is the accepted authority for liberal social faith.

spiritual but not religious

And the authority is good; for no one can read the words of Jesus honestly and not be shocked in turning to contemporary life. The salutary contrast has become a platitude; it even gets into the newspapers! We are not allowed to forget that our industrial system virtually says, Cursed are the poor, Cursed are the meek; that instead of turning the other cheek we hit back when we are struck, and far from overcoming evil with good, try to overcome it by more vigorous evil; that Christian manufacturers, instead of giving unto the last as unto the first, are likely to buy their labor as cheap as they can get it, and are often disposed to fight a living wage to the finish; that we do not fill the hungry with good things and assuredly do not send the rich away empty. The permanent contradiction between Christian morals and world-morals is a puzzle, and a permanent disgrace.

But even while stressing this contradiction, social Christianity needs another line of attack. For the radicalism which feeds wholly on such contrasts is ill-nourished, and in disgust with the Church is likely to slip away from Christ. We need to find in Christianity not only precept but dynamic, not only moral teaching but a revelation of God's actual dealings with men. Despite anti-dogmatic prejudice and anti-clerical revolt, despite an alignment which for the past hundred years or more has thrown the forces of progress largely on the non-Christian side, the real source of sound social philosophy must be sought, not only in the Teaching of Christ but in His Person; and, for the Christian, Christ is interpreted aright in His Mystical Body.

In the flow of the Church Seasons, Christian experience is revealed as a living thing, based on historic facts; and dogma is shown to be, not a mass of abstract assumptions torn out of life, but a transcript of realities as encountered by the soul. By these realities, all social phenomena must be measured. Unless our rising faith in social equality, in industrial democracy, in internationalism, be rooted in Catholic truth, one of two things will happen: either that truth will be discredited, or the social creed professed by liberals the world over will suffer defeat. For the Christian radical, neither alternative is conceivable. He believes that the amazing harmony between Christian truth and the new order is waiting to be discovered; and he is quite sure that only from the roots of a Christian and Catholic civilization could bloom the fair flower of a cooperative commonwealth, for whose unfolding we watch and pray.

This little book proposes then to study the social

implications of the Church Year under the guidance of the Book of Common Prayer. The method
will be a consecutive interpretation of the Sacred
Seasons, usually combined with meditation on the
social suggestions of the Epistles and Gospels
from week to week. The passages in the nature
of specific commentary can best be followed by
those who read, Prayer-Book in hand, with a view
to private devotion or perhaps to class-work; for
it is hoped that the book may be a companion in
Bible-Classes. But such passages can easily be
skipped by people who do not care for close study
of this kind or who have no Prayer-Book by them;
they are independent of the general interpretation.

Let no one suppose that by the approach to the
great truths commemorated in successive seasons,
Christian ethics is overlooked. The Epistles and
Gospels for the seasons are ethical in their very
fibre; only, from Advent to Trinity, first stress
is put on doctrine. During these seasons, the
Church dwells primarily on the great facts of the
life of Christ, His coming, His incarnation, His
ministry, death, and resurrection, His sending of
the Spirit, His eternal glory in the unity of the
Godhead. The Gospels which record these facts
naturally take the lead, while the Epistles illustrate and apply. After Trinity, the emphasis
changes; development of Christian duty in the life

of the Church is to the fore. The key-note from week to week is therefore more likely to be found in the Epistle, and the illustration in the Gospel. This order, which places the apprehension of divine Mysteries before the quest of practical duty, is not now popular; but it is the deliberately chosen order of the Church.

Before starting to consider the Sacred Seasons it is well to note two points.

The first is, that the very existence of the Church Year as presented in the Prayer-Book, is a tremendous witness to the power of the social instinct. No better illustration exists of the vital continuity of a corporate life down the ages. The Church, the Beloved Community, is the instrument of this life at its best, and the heart of the Church is in her worship. To feel how true this is, it is only necessary to glance at the living, harmonious work of the devout Christian mind from generation to generation.

"The Collects, Epistles and Gospels are, with some exceptions, the same that had been appointed in the ancient use of the English Church."[1] The

[1] A New History of the Book of Common Prayer, Procter and Frere. Macmillan, 1919.
See also, The Prayer-Book Interleaved, Campion and Beamont. Rivingtons, 1876. This book has been of great value throughout the following study.

basis of the arrangement is the "Comes," Companion, or Handbook, traditionally ascribed to St. Jerome early in the fifth century; but the more direct source is the Sarum Missal, or, at a still earlier date, the Missal of Leofric, tenth century Bishop of Exeter. The Reformation, however, which simplified so much in the over-rich liturgical growth of the later Middle Ages, also added much. We owe to the sixteenth century reformers certain of our most beautiful collects, as for example those for the first and second Sundays in Advent, that for the second communion on Christmas Day (the collect for the first communion is from the ancient mass of the Christmas vigil), those for Quinquagesima, Ash-Wednesday, the first Sunday in Lent and All Saints. These noble prayers, which take their place so naturally in the sequence, certainly testify to the spiritual fervor and sound Catholicity of the Reformers. The Scottish Church gives us the collect for Easter Even, and an American divine, Dr. Huntington, added to the fifteenth century Feast of the Transfiguration one of the most exquisite collects in the Prayer-Book. There could hardly be a fuller expression of organic human fellowship than this long story. For the true social instinct looks not only around, but back. It unites men, not only to the comrades of their own day, but to the vast majority who have passed beyond the touch of sense though not beyond the touch of faith. Time and space can not bind it; it can be satisfied with nothing short of the whole Communion of Saints.

The first social gift of the Church Year is then the initiation into a great brotherhood; and the second is the searching social discipline afforded by the observance of the Seasons.

The Puritans discarded this discipline, not only because it was Popish in their eyes, but because it was social. To their extreme individualism, the summons to rejoice all together on the twenty-fifth of December or to grieve all together on a special Friday, seemed unreal and formal. A human instinct led them, to be sure, to invent new forms of social expression, like Thanksgiving Day; but their aversion to the Feasts and Fasts of the Church lingered tenaciously till well within the memories of our own time.

But all Churches, not only those subject to bishops, are now realizing the helpful glow of these collective experiences, and are adopting the great Catholic days and seasons. This is because we are really growing more fraternal, and like to share our life much as a family might. Men are finding out, moreover, that the power so to share emotion releases rather than inhibits personality. When is a man most fully himself? When

has his spirit been most strongly fulfilled in glad-
ness or desire? Less often in solitary exaltation
than at times when consciousness has been swept
onward and upward by "one common wave of
hope and joy, lifting mankind again." Thousands
knew such absolution and enrichment of being
during the Great War: purified, freed, enlarged in
their whole manhood or womanhood, by sharing
a nation's life. Whether in sober or catastrophic
times, the wisdom of the Church steadfastly supplies such experience, through the epic cycle of
her Year. No military drill can surpass that
discipline in its power to secure inward solidarity.
How good it is for us! If sorrow befalls at
Christmas, what comfort to rejoice that Love is
born among men! If joy comes on Ash-Wednesday, how steadying the restraint of accepting our
share in the penitence of a sinful world! By so
merging personal mood and circumstance in the
universal emotion of Christendom, there is in-
calculable gain in subtle spiritual courtesy. Nor
can many more effective means be found for escap-
ing the self-centredness which is nowhere more
a curse than in the religious life.

And look at the matter, further, from the point
of view, not of the individual but of the community. Are we not coming to feel that in one
way or another, the Catholic ideal which subordi-

nates personal to general emotion, is needed by the modern state? Mechanical and automatic subjection to authority is bad, whether in state or Church; but voluntary self-control, born of imaginative sympathy, is the first qualification for democracy. A loving obedience to the will of Mother Church as she calls her children to follow the successive phases of her dramatic sequence, can furnish powerful aid in forming the interior habits which must be the strength of a socialized civilization. Our national life needs nothing so much as a sense of unity; and unity worth having can not be imposed from without or above, imperialisms to the contrary notwithstanding. It must flow forth from the spiritual organism into the political.

In our irresponsible and individualistic democracy, the value of the regulating and fusing power afforded by Catholic tradition, must be evident to every thoughtful Churchman; and his recognition of this value can add a patriotic stimulus to the passion with which he tries to use and share his privileges. Of course, the observance of the Christian Seasons is only one aspect of the corporate Catholic life; but it is a dramatized aspect which appeals to every man, woman and child. Enhanced fidelity in the observance might be one useful way of easing the transition from an in-

dividualistic society where every man is cheer-
fully fighting and feeling "on his own," to the
socialized democracy where every man shall discover his true freedom, in the harmony of fellowship.

This socialized democracy may be coming sooner
than we think. When it arrives, its citizens may
well recognize that qualities most conducive to the
health and peace of their politico-industrial existence result from the training offered by the ever-
changing, ever-renewed corporate experience of
the Christian Mysteries. The Catholic life should
normally be the soul of the democratic state.

CHAPTER I: THE SEASON OF ADVENT

Antiphon: When ye see these things, know ye that the kingdom of heaven is nigh at hand.

V. It is high time to awake out of sleep.

R. For now is our salvation nearer than when we believed.

Almighty God, give us grace that we may cast away the works of darkness, and put upon us the armour of light, now in the time of this mortal life, in which Thy Son Jesus Christ came to visit us in great humility; that in the last day, when He shall come again in His glorious majesty to judge both the quick and the dead, we may rise to the life immortal, through Him Who liveth and reigneth with Thee and the Holy Ghost, now and ever.   Amen.

CHAPTER I: THE SEASON OF ADVENT

ADVENT is a paradoxical season; like a College commencement, it registers a beginning as well as an end. In the mystic spiral of Christian experience, Trinity-tide gathers up and applies the lessons so far learned, and naturally develops a craving for future revelations yet to be. Year by year, Advent satisfies this craving, and is welcomed by faithful hearts with a sense of relief. In the quaint words of the old hymn, we rise to stretch our wings and trace our better portion. Our imagination is eagerly quickened, and we hear with exhilaration the solemn trumpet-call, "It is high time to awake out of sleep."

The season is at once retrospective and prophetic; it looks backward to the Incarnation, forward to the Day of Doom, and within these two Comings of God in humanity, His Coming as the Child and as the Judge, is implicitly comprised all relation of Christ to His world. Christianity is an historic religion, and in Advent the historic sense is particularly strong. Christianity is also a philosophical and ethical religion, and in Advent the initial principles which should define the Christian attitude are sharply brought out into light. From either point of view, the message of the season is threefold. It is a message of[1] Change, it is a message of the[2] Kingdom of God, and it is a message of[3] Judgment.

The message of Change is patent. The first social lesson of the Christian Year is that of life's perpetual flux. Movement, not stability, is the law of the Christian life, and of God's self-revelation in history. This is a fact important to realize at the outset; for our instinct is often to stay put, and to envisage change with distrust and dread; while the fundamental method of the Church is to keep us steadily, as Maeterlinck says we should be kept, in the light of a great expectation. The first thing she does with us is to turn us to face the future.

Institutional religion is constantly criticized as being formal, static, ultra-conservative. And no liberal can deny that the criticism is partly just, when he remembers the impenetrable wall of opposition to social developments which the Church has often presented; indeed, it suffices him to recall the rôle of organized religion during the Great War. It is good for the liberal to curb his impatience by recognizing the legitimate reason for this tendency. As every Catholic knows, the Institution preserves a mystic impulse at its heart; it exists to offer in a world of change the sure refuge of contact with eternity; and when men gain power to "break through" into this refuge, they are very likely at first to lose their sense of instability and their interest in motion. Now it is restful to find in religion an eternal calm; but if we read the Scriptures aright, we realize that it is fallacious. For legitimate rest is found, not in cessation but in the harmonious rhythms of growth; and the true Eternity in which the religious man consciously abides is no majestic frozen pause, but an unfolding life that flows forever from the Divine. Our God is today a God known to us only in process. We are forever children of process ourselves, and we would better frankly carry our evolutionary ideas over into our relations with the Eternal, and neutralize that dangerous old impulse to stiffen in our minds as soon as we become religious.

Be this as it may, the conservative habits of organized religion find scant sanction in the authoritative life and teaching of the Church: the cycle of Christian experience starts with solemn emphasis on the warning note of perpetual change; and there is a revolutionary quality to Advent emotion.

The first Collect, repeated every day till Christmas, is the dominant of the season. In magnificent cadences, it spans the whole course of Christian history, and faces us toward the eternity which lies beyond. No one who prays it can run contented, squirrel-wise, in his round. It generates at once the temper of noble excitement.

The Epistle for this first Sunday calls us back to sobriety; it opens with enumeration of plain moral duties summed up in the law of love. Christianity never fails in steadfastness and sanity, but neither does it ever stop with them; and all of a sudden, unexpectedly, St. Paul quickens our blood with the superb passage: ''Knowing the time, that now it is high time to awake out of sleep: for now is our salvation nearer than when we believed. The night is far spent, the day is at hand: let us therefore cast off the works of darkness, and let us put on the armor of light.'' In like manner, the second Epistle begins characteristically with warning us to be true to past tradition in all pioneer adventure; but loyalty to ''whatsoever things were written aforetime'' leads out instantly to hope, and to the exhilarating reminder that tradition exists to expand, and that the Gentiles are to rejoice with the Chosen People. The third and fourth Epistles find incentive to fidelity, in expectation of the time when the hidden things of darkness shall be brought to light, and the counsels of the hearts made manifest; and commend to the waiting soul the difficult union of joy and moderation, promising even to those whose eyes strain to the future age, the peace that passeth understanding.

Perhaps it is to emancipate us from the rigidity of one exclusive thought that the Church inaugurates her year with commemoration of a Coming not obviously distinctive of the season, and disconcerting at this point to the literal minded; the Gospel for the first Advent Sunday is the Entry into Jerusalem. Here, at all events, is a great fulfilment and also a great warning; for the Lord Whom we seek comes suddenly to His temple and purifies it in its shame. But the second Gospel sweeps us straight forward to the awful consummation of history. The third Gospel reminds us tenderly of the social emancipations which are ever the signs of the Coming of the Lord: "The blind receive their sight, and the lame walk, the lepers are cleansed, and the deaf hear, the dead are raised up, and"—climax even beyond the resurrection of the dead,—"the poor have the Gospel preached to them." The fourth Sunday gives us the Gospel of the Forerunner.

In all these Scriptures, as in the Lessons appointed throughout Advent for Morning and Evening Prayer, the emphasis is fully as social as it is personal. It is to the Church that St. Paul addresses himself. It is Israel the Chosen Nation which all the great prophetic utterances have in mind. Today, the Church and the nation, as well as the individual, should heed the call. If we enter into the spirit of the season, we shall escape all timid dread of change, all obstinate clinging to accustomed ways, in our own life or in the social order. That ''custom,'' which ''lies upon us with a weight heavy as frost and deep almost as life,'' will cease to press us down. Our temper will become alert, heroic, vigilant; ever earnestly watchful for the Signs of the Coming of the Son of Man.

It is as a King that Christ comes to the Daughter of Sion; and the next message of Advent is the message of the Kingdom. ''So likewise ye, when ye see these things come to pass, know ye that the Kingdom of God is nigh at hand,'' says the second Gospel. This very political Gospel looks directly forward to the mystic future when the Kingdom shall triumph visibly; the third Gospel carries us back to those happy days of the Galilean Ministry when the Lord preached to the poor the Glad News of the Kingdom of Heaven. And so the season calls us to contemplate that Kingdom, at once as solemn promise for the Golden Age to come, and as blessed reality here and now, in so far as the faithful follow their Master in His healing and releasing work for suffering men.

The Bible emphasis on the Kingdom of God is so impressive, so central, that one marvels how the Church could drop it out of her mind, as she did during long centuries. Perhaps the greatest religious gain of our own day is the rediscovery of this "dear truth," as Dr. Rauschenbusch loved to call it. Our social age has naturally discerned it in the Scriptures, for the Word of God has inexhaustible treasures, to meet distinctive and successive needs. But the social conception of the Kingdom, which has rapidly taken possession of Christian minds, has two groups of thoughtful opponents.

The first group includes those older thinkers who desire either to identify the Kingdom with the Church, or to construe it in a purely inward sense. And it would seem that neither interpretation stands the test of close modern study of the text of Scripture. To compress the ideal of the Kingdom within the actualities of the historic Church is a feat which few can perform; it is clear that the mind of Jesus enshrined the vision of a fellowship which the Church has rarely approximated, and of which it is at best an imperfect instrument. On the other hand, no modern scholar holds that the individualistic conception exhausts the thought as it lay in the Holy Mind. It is surely true that the Kingdom is "within" or "among" us; it is "righteousness, peace, joy in the Holy Ghost." But Jesus inherited the rich national ideal of a coming Reign of Justice on earth. He adopted the ideal to transform it, but only as He adopted to transform the Decalogue,— not by superseding, but by broadening and deepening.

While these older interpretations fade, absorbed in a stronger and wider thought, criticisms on the conception of the Kingdom emerge from another quarter. There is a growing distaste among some people for the beloved phrase. The meticulously-minded radical objects to talking about any Kingdom at all, even that of Heaven, and proposes to throw the expression on the scrap-heap, along with all those monarchical hymns which do certainly fail to meet the modern mind. Perhaps he may succeed; the Lord's ideal might conceivably be as well rendered by talking of the Republic of God, as of the Kingdom. It may be noted, however, that we shall probably continue to speak of the kingdom of Nature, the vegetable, animal and mineral kingdoms; and fussy people can continue to use the old term in this accredited sense with no violation of its true meaning, for the kingdom

indicated in the Sermon on the Mount is obviously
a supernatural order, governed by the influx of
new forces and developing new types; bearing in
a way much the same relation to the kingdom of
Nature as the animal kingdom bears to the mineral.

Most of us, however, shall remain satisfied to
use the old sacred wording in the old sacred sense,
—reminding ourselves, with Ruskin and Carlyle,
that while political kings may vanish, real king-
ship of the archetypal kind persists forever in
Heaven, and can never perish from the earth. We
thankfully recognize that, humanly speaking, the
establishment of the Kingdom of God was the purpose of Jesus' life. It is the constant theme of
all the swift dramatic changes recorded in the
Gospels; and the "note" of the Kingdom, first
struck in Advent, is naturally repeated in each
successive season of the Church's Year. The
Social Order born from above, the Beloved Community, already present in faithful hearts, but
shining in its full glory as the far goal of our
desire,—this, through all phases of penitence and
exaltation, of tragedy and triumph, the Church
never allows us to forget.

But the message of Change and the message of
the Kingdom alike find point and culmination

Social Teachings

out Advent in the message of Judgment; we can not rightfully apprehend either until we knit them into the great distinctive theme of the Season. It is the Coming of the Son of Man which shall inaugurate that glorious Day when the righteous shall shine forth as the sun in the Kingdom of the Father; it is the awed expectation of that Coming which detaches the Christian from tenacious clinging to established things, and makes, or should make, an evolutionist of him. The Church, in the great Advent Collect, keeps daily before our minds "the last Day when He shall come again in His glorious majesty to judge both the quick and the dead"; and through Gospels and Epistles to the very end of the season, the Apocalyptic hope of the Early Church, the definite expectation of the Coming in Judgment of the Son of Man, shines clear.

What does this hope mean to us,—Christians of the Twentieth Century,—anything at all?

Very little, it may be feared. Except for small groups here and there, effective belief in the Second Advent has by tacit consent dropped out from the mind of the Church. Mechanical interpretations have discredited it in any literal form, and in such form it is not likely to recur among educated people. That old vision of the dead, small and great, standing before God, the vision celebrated in the solemn rhythms of the Dies Iræ, painted by Orcagna and Michelangelo, haunts us no longer. It was replaced for a time by belief in an individual judgment occurring at death, but this conception too has failed; for few people probably now believe in a probation which ends when we leave the body. Judgment, to the modern man, is no longer a solemn climax, placed in the future; it is continuous process going on now; it is part of the ceaseless weaving of the web of life.

"Is there but one Day of Judgment?" writes John Ruskin. "Why, for us every day is a Day of Judgment—every day is a Dies Iræ and writes its irrevocable verdict in the flame of its West. Think you that judgment waits till the doors of the grave are opened? It waits at the doors of your houses,—it waits at the corners of your streets; we are in the midst of judgment—the insects that we crush are our judges—the moments we fret away are our judges—the elements that feed us, judge, as they minister—and the pleasures that deceive us, judge as they indulge." [1]

How spiritual this is, how beautifully put, how true! And yet at the same time it is quite inadequate from the point of view of Scripture. New Testament writers hold relentlessly before us the vision of a Judgment not only continuous but

[1] Ruskin: The Mystery of Life and its Arts.

catastrophic, not only present but future, not only personal but corporate. The Church, in stressing the same unpopular thought at the opening of her sequence of Christian experience, is merely loyal to the Bible. There can be no lack of precision in her language; it is almost melodramatic:—

"Grant that the ministers and stewards of Thy mysteries may likewise so prepare and make ready Thy way, by turning the hearts of the disobedient to the wisdom of the just, that at Thy second Coming to judge the world we may be found an acceptable people in Thy sight."

The faithful Churchman can hardly be content to let the whole difficult matter slip from his mind, and go on, year after year, singing hymns and praying prayers in which he does not believe. Has the social interpretation any help to offer?

In answering this question, it is well to keep in mind what was suggested at the outset. Every phase of the Christian Year has a double emphasis. It celebrates events, it also reveals principles. So, the Coming of Christ is conceived as a definite event; it is also conceived as an abiding law with recurrent manifestations. And probably the best way to get the right attitude toward the Church teaching concerning Judgment is to begin with the latter aspect.

Few things are more important than to restore

to the Christian mind the recognition that Jesus regarded catastrophe, no less than growth, as a normal and necessary element in human advance. He knew that violent disturbances were the condition and the preliminary of His Coming. We can not keep one factor in His teaching and reject another, dwell on the parable of the seed growing secretly, and forget the lightning flash. The Apocalyptic note is struck too clearly and persistently to be attributed to His reporters, or to later editors of His words.

Modern times have fought shy of accepting the religious necessity of violent change. They have prated much of Progress and Uniformity, of the gradual character of Nature's processes, and have turned away with deep distaste from any forces likely to create a disturbance. The cruder evolutionary ideas of the last century greatly helped this illusion of unbroken progress; for illusion it is, and it can not stand the light of reality. Philosophy is disillusionizing the thinker, and the grim facts of the last decade have been disillusionizing the man in the street. Still we believe in a Reign of Law, but the Law does not work in the fixed and placid way we have assumed; its manifestation in nature and history does not exclude, but includes, cataclysm. Earthquake and revolution are a part of it, as truly as sunrise and ordered social life. Moreover, the shock and agony, the overthrow of the usual and the normal, when sea and waves are roaring and the powers of Heaven are shaken and men's hearts fail them for fear, are a special revelation of the Eternal, without which His dealings with men were incomplete.

This is what Hebrew intuition had long seen; this is what Jesus, heir of that intuition, stressed; and this, of a certainty, is the permanent and sure truth which emerges profitably for us from the clouded Apocalyptic Teaching. Doubtless the Master believed that such fearsome, sudden revelation of the Judgment of God was part of the Divine Purpose and sure to occur within the historic order. The disciples caught His meaning; and they had no difficulty in making the political application to the affairs of their own day. Who shall say that they were wrong when in the phenomena surrounding the fall of their beloved Jerusalem they discerned the fulfilment of prophecy, one episode in the Judgment of God? Are not the same signs to be observed by us in the fall of Germany,—and by our children, conceivably, in the fall of this entire Western civilization of ours? What is important is that in each of these crises we should recognize no hideous accident, but the signs of the Advent of the Divine Humanity, of that Son of God Who is also the Son of Man.

Sudden, terrifying judgment on whole epochs and whole civilizations is a recurrent fact; and a fact which the Christian should prepare for and accept without aggrieved surprise. Catastrophe does not necessarily mean disaster, and tranquillity is not necessarily a blessing. The lesson is practical and pertinent; for we are passing through an Epoch of Judgment today, and we Christians shall miss its meaning if we resent it or try to suppress or hold it back, clinging to our complacent fallacies about Law and Order. We are not permitted to condemn a Russian Revolution, a Great War, or the I. W. W., merely because they are, on the surface, destructive and disturbing; they may be of the ordained Signs foretold.

There is great need here to clarify our thought. Obviously, Christians must do all in their power to avert disaster by the energies of constructive justice, and by the release of sacrificial love; they must, today, use every moment of grace granted them in this manner. And it is certainly not within the Christian scope to endorse methods of violence or bloodshed, far less to promote them.[1] To preserve ancient sanctities is part of religious duty; St. Paul's respect for constituted authority has a precious element in it, so far as external

[1] So at least one would suppose, if all through history the Church had not encouraged war, for causes she thought just.

behaviour goes, and the non-resistant factor in Christian ethic is indubitable.

Two points, however, must be noticed. The first is, that honest Christians, however far they be from aggressive revolutionaries, are always getting mixed up with them: the apostles are ar raigned as the men who turn the world upside down, and their Master is accused as one who stirs up the people; the misunderstanding is inherent in the situation, and will always persist. And the second point is that the Christian, while he neither endorses nor promotes revolution, will not hold the conventional attitude toward it when it comes. He knows that it is largely the index to his own past failure, his own bitter sin, and no resentment can stir within him against those who are the unconscious instruments of the Divine Judgment. Moreover, his holy faith enables him to recognize in man's failure, God's opportunity. Holy Writ and historic studies combine to convince him that life is never unbroken peaceful advance onward and upward. Turmoil and upheaval, war and revolution, are a part of the Divine Purpose "Distress of nations, with perplexity,—men's hearts failing them for fear, and for looking after those things which are coming on the earth,"—could there be a more exact description of the situation faced today? But in all these phenomena, the devout soul may be called to see the promise and precursors of the Coming of the Son of Man.

And if once we accept this difficult attitude, an astonishing thing happens: we rise to a new level of hope and joy. Advent is a penitential season, but it is not a pessimistic one. The Advent Scriptures, rightly read, are full of paradoxical exultation. Horror is heaped on horror in those descriptions of coming Doom which men in every world-upheaval,—never more than now,—have read with awed perception of their accuracy. What in such crises is the attitude enjoined on Christ's lovers? Are they to cower, passive, waiting with submissive dread for that which shall befall?— No; just the contrary: "Then look up, and lift up your heads; for your redemption draweth nigh."

"And He spake to them a parable: Behold the fig tree, and all the trees: when they now shoot forth, ye see and know of your own selves that summer is now nigh at hand. So likewise ye, when ye see these things come to pass, know ye that the Kingdom of God is nigh at hand."[1] Did it seem strange to the disciples,—this likening of distress, perplexity and fear, to the push of tender

[1] From the Gospel for Advent II.

leaves in Spring? The Master knew whereof He spoke: the times of Judgment are the Springtides of the world.

The spirit with which we anticipate judgment, personal or national, is a severe test of character. Do we shiver and evade? Or do we really want above all objects of desire that Truth be manifest, no matter how cruel and relentless the manifestation may be? If the purple hangings of our Advent betoken a real penitence, we shall welcome the test and crave the coming doom. Today, such welcome is in the air, among those detached from self-interest, whose hearts are set in the Eternal. They who have suffered with the world's slow hidden pain, consumed with anguish over the oppressions and corruptions which have poisoned modern life at the root, breathe a deep breath of relief as the old social order totters to its fall. What care they if dividends cease, though to their personal inconvenience? What if it should come to pass that private profit were socialized, and classes merged through tumult and struggle, in one great class of men laboring as a brotherhood? The release of passion, the bitter conflicts, the revelation of vicious selfishness in opposite quarters,—these are harder to endure: worse by far than any dislocation in outward things. But even here, the Christian, grieving as he must,

hope

can give thanks that evil is no longer suppressed, smoothed over, but out in the open, where love may perhaps reach it as never before. He can face catastrophe with confidence, because below all his penitence and shame is faith in both man and God. Judgment, salvation,—the terms are almost interchangeable throughout the Advent Scriptures.

St. Paul says an amazing thing in the Epistle for the third Sunday. He is making a practical application of the Master's precept and permission not to judge. Judge nothing before the time, says Paul,—advice which may, incidentally help us not to be doctrinaire about our economic judgments. Wait until the Lord comes. He will make manifest the counsels of the heart. "And then," —one feels that one can hardly have read the words aright,—"then shall every man have praise of God." Can that be really true? When hidden things are revealed, shall we find that men are better than we knew? Shall each and all deserve praise from the Holy God? Perhaps of "the self-same truth" we are all "foeman vassals." What a glorious end of our fierce struggles with one another in the darkness! Welcome Judgment if such is to be the result of it! Optimism could no further go.

Judgment then must be accepted by Christians

as an abiding principle. They must prepare for
it by constant watchfulness, and they must welcome it when it comes, though the very foundations of their social life be shaken. Can we go
further than this? Can the faithful of the twentieth century gain any good from the older, more
literal interpretation? Are we moderns still able
to anticipate judgment, not only as recurrent manifestation of law, but as one great future Event,
the goal of history?   *Global Warming*

The question is too tremendous for humble lay
minds to approach with hope of dogmatic solution.
Apart from other difficulties, we are at once con-
fronted, from the social point of view, by the fact
that belief in the Second Coming has usually carried with it an unsocial fatalism. It has encouraged a mystical aloofness from earthly life, it
has cut the nerve of reform. The many modern
thinkers who frankly call Christian ethic impossible, like to point out that it was conceived as a
mere *ad interim* policy, suitable only for a swiftly
passing world-order which would hardly survive
one generation. Clever debaters enjoy countering
this way scornfully, when Christian procedure is
urged on them; and devout believers have often
been lured by similar convictions to run away,
metaphorically at least, into monasteries, and to
leave the poor world to its fate.

We do not want to identify ourselves with either set of minds; yet neither do we want to dodge the issue. Jesus told us to pray, "Thy kingdom come on earth." He never would have enjoined on us a prayer which could not be answered; and by very law of holy obedience, we are bound therefore to believe that the kingdom will come.

The Scriptural treatment of the Second Advent is of course entwined with that millennial hope of the Jews, so alien to modern thought. It is identified with a Messianic faith. All New Testament writers look forward to the Coming of the Lord as to a great historic event, no less concrete than His birth. Perspective lengthens as the years pass between the earlier and the later books of the Canon; but there is never any doubt as to what the end will be.

Now the Messiah is to most people today a conception which has ceased to interest; and those who see in Jesus, not so much the moral teacher as the more or less fanatical heir of an Apocalyptic tradition, are inclined to place Him among the visionaries whose fallacies have misled the ages. Yet the Catholic mind can not dispense with either aspect of the Lord's Teaching. We have no right to ignore the depth and cogency of Apocalyptic prophecy; far less can we ignore the clear assurance of all New Testament writers and of Jesus

Himself, that this prophecy shall find its last fulfilment in His Advent to judge the past and to
initiate a mystic future.

Beyond this point, Christian thought will always
diverge. We may be pre-Millenarians, looking
forward to a cataclysm in the middle of earth-
history, when Christ shall return and summon His
saints—and nobody else—to live and reign on
earth a thousand years; we may be post-Millenarians, thinking an Advent at the end of the life
of this planet to be more likely. Discussion between the pre- and post-Millenarians is going on
vigorously today. To the plain Christian, it
usually seems that the pre-Millenarians are caught
in the toils of materialistic literalism, while the
post-Millenarians often lose any sense of reality
at all. But of course both schools are intent on the
same tremendous fact, which their discussions
sometimes obscure. And any effective belief in
this fact must evoke a special quality in the
Christian's feeling and behaviour. To be in-
fluenced in one's life, either outward or interior, by an indefinite expectation, however
sure, needs imagination; it is a test, and
a difficult one. But people who possess "the substance of things hoped for" ought to stand that
test. The man who really believes that the Love

of God, revealed in the Incarnate Word, is to
be mightily and openly manifest in history as the
measure by which the race shall be judged, can not
feel or act like other men.

[handwritten: What do you believe?]

"This Advent moon shines cold and clear, *[handwritten: I agree,]*
   These Advent nights are long; *[handwritten: and yet I]*
Our lamps have burned year after year, *[handwritten: struggle w/]*
   And still their flame is strong. *[handwritten: what that will look like]*
'Watchman, what of the night?' we cry, *[handwritten: Revelations?]*
   Heart-sick with hope deferred: *[handwritten: Jesus coming]*
'No speaking signs are in the sky,' *[handwritten: on the clouds?]*
   Is still the watchman's word.

The Porter watches at the gate,
   The servants watch within;
The watch is long betimes and late,
   The prize is slow to win.
'Watchman, what of the night?' but still
   His answer sounds the same:
'No daybreak tops the utmost hill,'
   Nor pale our lamps of flame.

One to another hear them speak,
   The patient virgins wise:
'Surely He is not far to seek,—
   All night we watch and rise.

The days are evil looking back,
    The coming days are dim;
Yet count we not His promise slack,
    But watch and wait for Him.' " '[1]

Shall this watching and waiting be merely passive? Is it logical that the more vividly people image to themselves the great Coming, the less interested they are in earthly affairs? A real temptation lurks here. If this great End of History, is sure, quite apart from our purposes and struggles, are men not justified in their other-worldliness, in their cloisters?

Not in the least, according to the Scriptures. The virgins are to fill their lamps with oil before they slumber and sleep in death; the servants are to work hard multiplying their talents, the laborers are to be active in the vineyard. All the parables which relate to the Judgment stress activity in a perfectly normal way. And the very Millennial conception, if one thinks it through, carries with it a tremendous social appeal.

For the Millennium was the Hebrew and Early Christian Utopia, and it is therefore not out of place for us to claim Christian sanction for a Utopian hope. We shall be helped to find the value of the idea in proportion as we import real-

[1] Christina Rossetti.

ism into our conception of the Kingdom of Heaven. We do not know when the gradual invisible growth of the Kingdom, illustrated in the parables of the Leaven and the Seed, will find its consummation in the flash of lightning which heralds the Coming of the Son of Man. But when that end does come, we ought to be ready for it. The best way to watch is to prepare.

If there is really to be a better and holier society, following a great manifestation of the Judgment of God, human men and women will live in it. Therefore, the Church ought to be training her children now, today in millennial morals. For it is never the Lord's way to impose His laws on a passive people; His whole business with us is to train us to self-government. Paradise is sure to be democratic. All our civic intelligence, our power, still embryonic, to act harmoniously together, our practice of syndicalism, soviets, or guild socialism if you will, prepare us for citizenship in the Heavenly City. There will be no ''social service,'' one hopes, in that happy time, but there will be the cooperative commonwealth. Blessed citizens will have to run it, and those who are furthering justice and welfare now will be the most useful people then. It is not a bad test of one's occupations to ask whether one could go on with them in the Kingdom of Heaven. There

Cool !

will be plenty for Hoover to do in that heaven,—not feeding the starving, but organizing the food-supply of the race; it might prove harder to employ the barons of finance unless incentive alters.

And of Him Who said that He was coming back in His glory, with all His holy angels with Him, what can be said? Perhaps few Christian minds today dare take the words literally, and a frank confession of uncertainty is the most honest course. We are in the shadows where even the humblest orthodoxy must wait patiently for light.

But if Christian minds are uncertain, Christian hearts cling to that hope forever. It is permissible to be a little hazy about the Second Advent. No one can be as definite about the future as about the past, and Nazareth must be clearer to the Christian than the Day of Judgment. But we know that great Persons always stand at the focal points of history; and the greatest hour that history shall ever know will call for the appearance of One supremely great. Who can it be save One who loves to the uttermost, and who can reveal to men the eternal sacrifice of God? Only human nature can judge humanity; yet (experience shows the paradox to be essential) the human nature must possess absolute holiness, infinite wisdom.

We abide then, watching with passionate sober expectation for the Coming of that Love which man has crucified, to judge the race of man. In the courage of that expectation, our temper grows heroic. We face the future, released from convention or timidity; we welcome with no surprise, even with awe-struck joy, those historic upheavals which are the normal Sign of His approach. The man who is disciplined in the Blessed Hope of Advent may not be fatalist, may not be despondent. His happy heart is set to the music of the last canonical prayer of the Church: ''Even so come, Lord Jesus.'' And through whatever tragic anguish our piteous race may pass, he clings to the magnificent incontrovertible words of the Apostle: ''Now is our salvation nearer than when we believed.''

''The world about us, with its lawlessness, its disunions, its jarrings, seems sometimes as if it could attain to no great end; like a restless sea of many waters, aimless, barren, unprogressive. But there is purpose in it. The tossing sea we shall behold one day with the fires of the Divine Judgment, as St. John beheld it, 'a sea of glass mingled with fire,' and beyond the judgment again,

as the sea of glass clear as crystal which mirrors
in its calm surface the throne of God before which
it is spread. 'For though the waves toss themselves they shall not prevail.' All things move
on to the Divine Event. The nations of the earth
shall bring their glory and their honour into it.
All things in heaven and earth shall bow and adore
Jesus, the heir of the whole world's movement
and fruitfulness." [1]

We proceed on our journey,—but we do not
leave the Advent message behind. The method of
the Church is as human as it is profound. Each
new truth is remembered faithfully during all
sequences to come, invigorates its successors, and
blends with them harmoniously in the diapason
which shall close only in the Kingdom of Heaven.
The note of Change, the note of the Kingdom, the
note of Judgment,—they will be found persistent,
recurrent, interpenetrating the Christian consciousness more and more as other truths develop
to bear them company. Through the star-light of
Christmas, through the dawn of Easter, through
the noon-tide glory of Ascension, through the
flame of Pentecost, flashes the same summons:
"Behold, thy King cometh unto thee;" "Lift up
your heads; for your redemption draweth nigh."

[1] Bishop Gore: The Incarnation of the Son of God, p. 153.

CHAPTER II: CHRISTMAS-TIDE

Antiphon: That was the true Light, which lighteth every man that cometh into the world.

V. Glory to God in the Highest,

R. And on earth peace.

O God, Who makest us glad with the yearly remembrance of the birth of Thine only Son Jesus Christ; Grant that as we joyfully receive Him for our Redeemer, so we may with sure confidence behold Him when He shall come to be our Judge, Who liveth and reigneth with Thee and the Holy Ghost, one God, world without end.

Amen.

CHAPTER II: CHRISTMAS-TIDE

WHAT deep tenderness in the sequence by which Mother Church, having disciplined us in awe and pentitential hope, now leads to the Manger where Mary bends over the new-born Babe!

"God Who shinest from the Maid,
Have mercy upon us!"

The God for Whose Coming in judgment we have been at watch in dread and in desire, is no stranger. Flesh of our flesh, soul of our soul, helpless in babyhood, He holds out beseeching arms to Humanity His Mother, asking that we who have brought Him to the birth, should nourish and cherish Him. Dependent on us,—oh, mystic thought!—for the power to fulfil His purpose and to make us whole, He seeks our nurturing love that it may bring Him to the fullness of His Manhood:

"From the remembering flesh that in it bore
The thoughts of old dead peoples and their dreams,
I made Thee, O Lord.

From the flesh of the fool that laughing in his
    heart
Cried with an empty voice, There is no God,
        I made Thee, O Lord.

From our desire and from our mortal need,
From the prayer we raise and our delight in Thee,
        I created Thee, God.
And perished races, rising up in me,
Fashioned Thee wildly of my little dust,
And breathed upon Thy Face the image of man.
        I created Thee, God.'' [1]

Deity self-subjected to our mortal nature! One
dare not try to fathom the mystery. Even its
social implications are to be discerned only from
the posture of prayer.

But the first concern of the Church at this her
Festival is to hold clear before her children's
minds the whole process of experience on which
they have entered. Therefore, the beautiful Collect for the first Christmas Communion, from the
Mass of the Christmas vigil, binds into unity the
two seemingly so disparate Comings of God to
man.

In the Prayer-Book of 1549, provision was made
for two Communions at Christmas; and the In-

[1] Anna Hempstead Branch The Madonna of the Earth.

troit for the first Communion was Psalm 98, "O
sing unto the Lord a new song." The exultant
end of the psalm is as all remember, the prophecy
of judgment fulfilled in justice:

"Let the floods clap their hands and let the hills
be joyful together before the Lord; for He is
come to judge the earth. With righteousness
shall He judge the world and the people with
equity."

The Epistle, a somewhat unfamiliar passage
from Titus, strikes the same note. It really involves the whole Christian revelation: Incarnation, Atonement, and the active life of the Church,
that is of the "peculiar people, zealous of good
works." But the chief point made is that even in
the moment of fulfilment, when we hail salvation
manifest, we are to remain expectant, "looking
for that blessed hope, and the glorious appearing
of the Great God, and our Saviour Jesus Christ."

So delicately, so carefully, does Mother Church
make her transition. The link between Christmas
and Advent thus strongly forged, we turn, still
at the first Communion, to the Gospel of the
Nativity: the idyll of the ages, the poem of poems,
where visionary glory blends most perfectly with
human tenderness, and heaven and earth are one.

And the story begins in a very literal manner.
The historic background is defined: the Roman

rule, a Cæsar on the throne, the date fixed by a certain Cyrenius, Governor of Syria. And the reference to a census, of all things! Economic determinism if you please,—the materialistic interpretation of history,—a sordid fiscal phenomenon deciding to all outward seeming the birthplace of the world's Redeemer! Yet, prosaic though the opening and setting be, the tale itself in its divine simplicity is justly the heart of Christian song and art and worship. What, sentence by sentence, it means to the spirit, the faithful ponder in silence. The passage opens with decrees and taxes in an obscure subject province; it ends with the good tidings of a universal joy, with the angelic song announcing peace on earth to all men of good will. We are in the sphere of time and history; but the history has its inception in the secrets of eternity, and time is invaded by mysterious beauty from a world beyond its measurement.

So run the Scriptures appointed for the first Christmas Communion. Those for the second, the great Festal Eucharist, are quite different. The thought of judgment to come is ignored, neither have we any narrative of the Holy Birth in Judæa. Rather, we are transported wholly behind history and out of time. The Epistle, from the first chapter of Hebrews, lifts us to contem-

plation of the Eternal Sonship, wherein are fulfilled the most mystical ideals of the Jewish mind.
The supreme Gospel, opening of the Gospel according to St. John, final resultant of the con-
fluence of Hebrew emotion and of Greek philosophy, invites us to the contemplation of the
Eternal Word, that was with God and was God.
And as the worshippers kneel at the glorious consummation: "The Word was made Flesh and
dwelt among us," faith in the Incarnation, basis
of all social hope, as of all personal salvation, is
perfected within their hearts.

Whether we contemplate God Incarnate as the
Word or as the Babe, one central fact is clear.
Truth is not remote from us, not alien, not lost
to human sight in an Eternal Absolute; it is no
less our Child than our Saviour. So Newman
points out in the *Apologia* the special teaching
implied in the concept of the Madonna,—the
Truth "lying hid in the bosom of the Church as if
one with her, clinging to and as it were lost in her
embrace." For "Church" substitute "Humanity" and we have here recognition of the fact
which modern philosophers and popular writers,—
a Bergson, a Wells,—are heralded abroad for discovering; and like all sound human thinking about
God, it has long been familiar to the Catholic

mind. That mind has probably often entertained wrong ideas; but it has missed no vital idea, essential for full religious living. This evolving God, this God Whom man creates, Who waits on man for the full release of His power, this God to Whom our attitude may be not only filial but maternal, is in very truth the Second Person of the Ever-Blessed Trinity.

The Infinite woos us from every side, approaches us by every avenue of our complex nature. God above us, Creator, Monarch, Father, does not suffice our need: God within us, Comfort, Inspiration, Sustainer, leaves us still unsatisfied. To fulfil our desire, Infinite Love must yield itself utterly to our care, be dependent on us for shelter and nurture, be in awesome fact the Son of Man.

This aspect of reality is peculiarly evident today, and peculiarly appealing. Stark and ruthless experience presses home to thousands of hearts the old cruel dilemma between a callous and an impotent God. In this storm-racked world, it becomes no alternative to be considered in the calm of theologic studies, but a terrible choice to be made under fierce and open skies which look down brazenly on human anguish. And the imperious craving for a vision of the Eternal which every great moment of history lays bare, finds with many its best satisfaction in clinging to a Great Comrade Who was thwarted like us, Who is ever crucified with His own, helpless in large measure yet all the dearer for that helplessness. Such thinking could of course be final to no Christians; but it is true, though partial; and Christians may find their best comfort, by the Manger or the Cross, in contemplating the Absolute in process of becoming, the voluntary limitations of Omnipotence.[1]

And in such contemplation there is solemn incentive and summons. For if such be the law of the Manifestation of God in history, what re-

[1] The thought in the text is strikingly illustrated by a passage from a modern philosopher:

"Plato and Aristotle represented God as that absolute Good which, unmoving and changeless in Itself, the soul pursues and longs for. To Christianity, it is the soul that is pursued, and God is forever restless, in quest of what to him is lost. The God of the Christian is one who invades the earth in order to bring men to themselves: to every soul of man, he 'stands at the door and knocks.' He does not forego the power of silent attraction found in the non-assertive Tao of Lao-Tze, or in Brahm, or in the Unmoved Mover of the Greeks; but it is as one who has known finitude, and is 'lifted up from the earth,' that he will draw all men unto him. He disguises himself, takes the form of a servant; he comes to his own and his own know him not; he is despised and rejected and done to death. And all this is the foil and background of his great joy. For he has his moment when to some mind more honest than usual to its own need, there comes a presentiment of recognition, and the awed question, "Who art thou, Lord?"—to which he answers, "I am he whom thou persecutest." . . .

"If God exists as a good will, that will must do its work in the world of time and event as a will to power not wholly unlike our own, and so coming to itself, as we must, through the saving of others. Christianity is right in holding that such a God if he exists must somehow appear in the temporal order. And it seems

sponsibility is ours whose high office it is, like the Virgin Mother, to bring forever to the birth the Saviour of the world!

In the message of Christmas, mystical and social truth are one. This very day, as we talk of a "new social order," the Christ-child calls for our mothering. The spiritual ideal, which comes from Above, is sojourning indeed among men, but in what trembling infancy! Shame is attendant on its coming . . . (Do we think enough of what was involved to Mary in her "Ecce Ancilla Domini," of Joseph's distress, which deserved angelic comforting?) : there is a stigma on the Truth. It is not born among the rich of the earth, but among the lowly; it is denied our habitations, and waits outside, uncertain of our fostering. We may not go our careless way, thinking that God is strong enough to take care of Himself. He has chosen to be weak, to be a babe in our arms, Whom if we will we may dash against the stones. Alas! like the Old Masters who always introduced the

to me that it is also right in saying that he must suffer, and not alone with us (as any god must who knows what is going on), but also for us and at our hands. . . . It is such a god, active in history and suffering there, that Christianity declares as the most important fact about the world we live in.

"To believe in such a god would give history a meaning over and above any experimental meaning it may have: it would have to be read as the drama of God's life, his making and remaking of men."—Human Nature and Its Remaking. W. Ernest Hocking. Yale University Press, 1918.

symbols of the Passion into their sweetest Nativities, we must at Bethlehem remember Calvary.

So we worship the Divine, not withdrawn into its own purity, but identifying itself with an unfolding life within the natural order of history. And that fair and holy light of God shining from the Maid, quickens and illumines all our social efforts. Behold, the Tabernacle of God is with men. Housing reform, sanitation, dietetics and the like, are all sanctified by the Incarnation. A false spirituality often laments that the Churches turn to such matters; and indeed they are pernicious evasions of the essential truth, evidences of our materialistic age, if taken for a moment as ends in themselves. But to the true Christian, they are triumphant assertions of his faith in the Word made Flesh. Two forms of faithlessness are equally dangerous. One rests in natural good as a finality, the other dreads or despises it, drawn to the ever-barren quest for discarnate Spirit. Only the Catholic faith escapes these evils. Indifference to earthly life and satisfaction in it are alike denied to him who kneels before the Babe. To him, the world of sense is neither illusion nor enemy; but still less is it his object. It is the sacramental instrument of the Spirit, and he would fain ensure its health and purity with as anxious care as men show in preparation of the Eucharistic Host. All those labors, which seek for the race a healthful and decent physical existence, are preparations that men may be born from above; it is our high privilege to make the social organism a fit home for the Indwelling God.

It is good to dwell on the Joyful Mysteries of the Gospels, and it is happiness to linger with the dear associations which surround the childhood of the Lord.

Why did He not come as a Prince, whose dramatic laying aside of kingly rank and pomp might afford a noble object lesson? Such is the opening of the story of the Buddha, and no one can read the lovely tale without emotion. A similar image is not denied to the Christian: he has but to send his worshipping imagination back into eternity:

"Thou didst leave Thy throne and Thy kingly
    crown
When Thou camest on earth for me"—

Precious are such thoughts, but precious also to the Christian heart the symbols of which it never wearies: the Cave, the shepherds, and the friendly beasts, the homelessness of the Divine Babe, the brooding mother. Here is the Treasure of the Humble. Throughout Christian history, the poor

Beautiful

and lowly have found at the Manger the sweet revenge of secret laughter over the solemn pretensions of earth's mighty ones. Here they echo in murmured undertones which are never silenced, the amazing song which gives us our chief insight into the heart and mind of Mary the Hebrew woman:

"He hath put down the mighty from their seat and hath exalted the humble and meek. He hath scattered the proud in the imagination of their hearts. He hath filled the hungry with good things and the rich He hath sent empty away."

Old Langland puts it well in his fourteenth century vision of the Workman Christ,—the Ploughman who is to him the symbol and representative of the Redeemer:—

"To pastours and to poets appeared that angel,
And bade them go to Bethlehem, God's birth to
          honour,
And sung a song of solace, Gloria in Excelsis Deo.
Rich men (slept) then and in their rest were,
Tho it shone to the shepherds, a shewer of
          bliss." [1]

[1] Langland: The Vision of William Concerning Piers the Plowman. Ed Skeat. Passus xii, B. l. 150-153.

It is especially touching to penetrate tne hidden mind of the middle ages, that most aristocratic of periods. The Church shared the delight of the time in haughty external magnificence; and pictures rise before us of sacerdotal pomp, of arrogant prelates maintaining feudal state, of a Papal foot on an imperial neck. Yet the more one studies the suppressed emotions of the age and the strong undercurrents, the greater ferment of radical and democratic thought one discovers. It is largely generated by the Gospel story. St. Francis sits him down on the bare ground, weeping, as one of his brothers breaks into meditation on the hardships of the Saviour's birth. In the overt dignity of mosaic, fresco or sculpture, men might depict the Christ as King or Judge; within their private hearts they cherished another image, the image of the Workman, the lover of men, a wanderer from His birth, not knowing where to lay His head. As Langland writes again:

"For our joy and our heal Jesus Christ of Heaven
In a poor man's apparel pursueth us ever,
And looketh on us in their likeness, and that with
      lovely cheer." [1]

A quaint fourteenth century homily strikes gently and tenderly the same note:—

[1] Ditto. Passus xi, B. 1. 179-181.

"Now dere friend before matins sall thou thynke of the swete birthe of Jesus Christ alther first. The tyme was in mid-wynnter when it was maste cald, the hour was at mydnight, the hardeste hour that is, the stede was in mydwarde the streete, and in house withouten walles. In clouts was He bounden and in a crib before an oxe and asse that lufely Lord was laid, for there was no other stede voyde. Thou sall thynke also of the herdes that saw the token of His birthe, and thou sall thynke of the swete fellawschip of angels, and rayse uppe thy herte and synge with them, Gloria in excelsis Deo."[1]

In the miracle-plays, the "movies" of the middle ages if an irreverent comparison be permitted, the Holy Drama is triumphantly and audaciously brought within the mental compass of plain folk; and the results are often as charming as they are absurd. The treatment afforded far more than a chance for buffoonery; it sprang from the deep instinct to consecrate the roughest realities of working-class life, by the Presence of God sojourning with men. Therefore the shepherds shiver and grumble in their own distinctive dialect on English moors:—

[1] The Mirror of St. Edmund. C. Horstman. Richard Rolle of Hampolle I, 235. Swan Sonnenschein, 1895.

"I Pastor:

Lord, what! these weders are cold!   And I am ill-
    happed;
I am nere-hand dold, so long have I napped;
My legys thay fold, my fyngers ar chapped. . . .

But we sely shepardes that walkys on the moore,
In fayth, we are nere-handys out of the doore;
No wonder, as it standys, if we be poore,
For the tilth of our landys lies fallow as the floor
        As ye ken.
We are so hamyd,
For-taxed and ramyd
We are made hand-tamed
        With these gentlery men." [1]

The angelic message floats through bleak British
skies, interrupting the most realistic of horseplay.
Sometimes, the shepherds squabble over the words
of the ditty:

"Nay, it was glory, glory with a glo,
And much of Celsis was thereto."

But, reconciled, they seek the Manger, where the
art of Hogarth yields to that of Fra Angelico, and
the poets lavish all their lyric tenderness.   They

[1] Towneley Plays.   Secundus Pastorum.

worship their "lytell Daystarne" with appropriate gifts; now a bob of cherries or a spoon that will hold forty pease, now two cobb-nuts on a ribbon or a brooch with a tin bell. Always there is the same simplicity, the same half-sly, half-defiant insistence that the first welcome to the Blessed One came from homely working-folk. The Pageant of the Magi follows that of the Shepherds, but it has not half the charm.

> "The Vision of Christ which thou dost see
> Is my Vision's greatest enemy."[1]

So William Blake was to write, hundreds of years after the miracle-plays. The hieratic and monarchical instincts of the middle ages transformed the image of the Carpenter of Nazareth for the most part to their own likeness: but they never quite managed to get possession of the Baby.

All pastorals find their consecration in the exquisite idyll of the Nativity night; and throughout English letters, the graceful play of classic suggestion gains again and again a deeper, sweeter note, from the memory of those Hebrew shepherds to whom the skies were musical with holy song. But more than pastoral feeling centres

[1] Blake: The Everlasting Gospel.

here. Kneeling at the Manger, we are present at
the inception of the blessed associations with
normal labor, normal life, and primal emotion,
which pervade the Gospels. The Christian love
for children, the Christian reverence for the family, as well as the Christian tenderness toward
poverty,—here all these precious instincts are
born; to this shelter, when buffeted by the world,
they can always return.

The literal, simple meaning of the narrative is
the best and most important. But beyond or
within this meaning, the Christian imagination
has always loved to play with parables: —

"Wird   Christus   tausendmal   zu   Bethlehem
      geboren,
Und nicht in dir: du bleibst noch ewiglich verloren." [1]

So we may see in the shepherds the lowly motions
of the heart, in the angels the winged powers of
the soul, in the wise men the gifts of the intellect,—all gathered in love and worship at the
House of the Babe. Harmonious images, suggesting the full loveliness of redeemed human life,
centred in adoration of Eternal Love. But there
are shadows in the picture. Herod is not far

[1] Angelus Silesius.

away. Nor should we wish to discover within us the host who turned the Mother from the inn. Very likely he was not a bad man, that host. One fancies the crowds, hurrying at the law's behest to sign their income tax returns, so to speak, in their home town: the busy hour, the worried man, the casual irresponsible negative to a difficult appeal. He Who at the Last Day shall say, "Unto the least of these," warns us, when we fail to house the homeless, be it by private hospitality or by corporate care, Whom it is we leave unsheltered:—

"Whether my house is dark or bright,
I close it not on any night,
Lest Thou, hereafter King of stars,
Against me close Thy heavenly bars.

"If from a guest who shares thy board,
Thy dearest dainty thou shalt hoard,
'Tis not that guest, oh, do not doubt,
But Mary's Son shall do without."[1]

Society, all too often, it is to be feared, plays the part of the host.

The Feasts which cluster around Christmas were appointed at different times. That of St.

[1] Collection of Irish verse.

Stephen dates as far back as the fourth century, that of St. John is first mentioned in the Mozarabic missal of the sixth; it is uncertain when the formal commemoration of the Holy Innocents began, though Origen says that their Memorial was celebrated in Churches after the manner or order of the saints. By the twelfth century, St. Bernard mentions the three as one connected commemoration following Christmas. And they belong there quite beautifully, for they recall the three aspects of the Lord of Glory so far stressed by the Church Year: Christ the Son of God, High Priest and Intercessor; Christ the Eternal Word, Christ the Babe of Bethlehem.

We recall the first Christmas Epistle from Hebrews, as we read the vision of the protomartyr; for it is the Son ''Whom He hath appointed heir of all things, by Whom also He made the worlds,'' Whom Stephen sees ''standing on the right hand of God.'' The Feast of St. John, he who is in fullest sense evangelist of the Incarnation, could be placed nowhere except by the Manger; the Epistle for the day echoes the great Prologue associated with John's name, which is the central light of our Christian devotions; in its reiterated stress on the contact of hands and ears and eyes with the very Word of Life, it links the thought of the mystical and of the historic Christ together.

As for the Holy Innocents, they bring us back
into history again. Patrons of all child-sufferers,
they are always thought of near the Christ-Child,
for whom unconsciously they died, and whom,
according to a sweet old legend, their little mar-
tyred spirits guard on the Flight into Egypt.
Nothing could illustrate better than the position
of these Feasts the wise instinct of the Church,
and the remarkable suggestiveness for devout
hearts of her seemingly most fortuitous sequences.

And when the Feasts are over, the Scriptures
for the first Sunday after Christmas and for the
Circumcision complete the golden ring in which
they are enclosed, by bringing us back to the Manger. St. Joseph, who has no special Feast-Day in
our Communion, certainly has as much right to
be there as St. Stephen or the Innocents, and it is
well for us to hear how to that "just man" is
given the privilege of announcing the name of
the Saviour. It is after the first touch of human
pain, as the Circumcision Gospel tells, that the
Name is finally bestowed. Meanwhile, the two
Epistles, as is their wont, connect the practical
life of the Christian and the Church with the
Mysteries chronicled in the Gospels. We too,
through the Son, have received the adoption of
sons, and the spirit that cries "Abba, Father";

and finally the Epistle for the Feast of the Circumcision, facing straight toward Epiphany, asserts the splendid truth that the Christmas light reaches to all the horizons of the world —the blessedness of life renewed in purity being proclaimed by the Apostle to be the heritage of uncircumcised as of circumcised, of Gentile as of Jew.

CHAPTER III · THE SEASON OF EPIPHANY

Antiphon: The fellowship of the mystery from the beginning of the world hath been hid in God.

V. We have seen His star in the east,
R. And are come to worship Him.

O God, Who by the leading of a star didst manifest Thy only-begotten Son to the Gentiles; Mercifully grant that we, who know Thee now by faith, may after this life have the fruition of Thy glorious Godhead; through Jesus Christ our Lord.

Amen.

CHAPTER III: THE SEASON OF EPIPHANY

ADVENT celebrates the expectation of the Truth, Christmas the coming of the Truth; Epiphany, the ancient Feast of Lights, celebrates the discovery or manifestation of the Truth. Since manifestation is progressive and gradual, the season is long. Epiphany was the original Feast of the Incarnation, and for a long time commemorated a fourfold glory: the Birth, the Star, the Baptism, and the Marriage at Cana. "Thou Who didst make the world wast manifested in the world, to enlighten those who sat in darkness. Glory to Thee, O lover of men." So runs a short hymn of the Greeks. And again, another Greek hymn: "O Christ, the true light which lighteth every man that cometh into the world, let the light of Thy countenance be shown upon us, that thereby we may behold the light which is unapproachable, and guide our steps to fulfil Thy commandments."

It is a very shining season, and a very adventurous one.

The opening of it finds us still at the Manger.

Labor was there first, in the persons of the shepherds, but Wisdom follows soon. It comes from very far, but it has heavenly guidance. Perhaps one would rather be led by an angel than a star, but a star is not to be despised.

The Epistle of the Feast-Day gives the keynote of the season: the expanding revelation of the large inclusiveness of love, which is an open mystery like all-embracing light. That those outside the Circumcision should be of the initiate was a marvellous thing, a mystery indeed, to the apostle. Exclusiveness marked all possession of truth in the ancient world. The Jews had no dealings with the Samaritans; in the cults of the great mystery-religions, to which Paul here refers, the esoteric revelation was so jealously guarded that we still speculate about it. A Mystery was to be protected from all breath of the outer world. But the Christian Mystery was of a different character; and Paul found a pregnant phrase to describe it. Ours is "the *fellowship* of the Mystery,"—fellowship limitless, unconditioned, in that true light which lighteth every man that cometh into the world. That the Gentiles should be fellow-heirs, of the same Body, and partakers of the promise in Christ,—here is a mystery indeed, only to be made known by revelation, then and now. Fellowship! It is a great

Christian word: fellowship is heaven, the lack of it is hell.

If our social order is to reproduce the spiritual order which is in Christ, it must sweep all separateness away. The Manifestation of the divine life, in the secular as in the religious world, can tolerate no guarded privilege.

The special Manifestation on which the Church dwells during this holy season, is of course that of the ministry of Christ on earth. Swiftly the precious Sundays pass, touching in light suggestion on the chief phases of the Holy Life. The not inconsiderable modern school which thinks the death of Christ to be as it were incidental, and bids us look not to the death but to the life for salvation (as if that unity could be dissevered which is the complete revelation of Deity in Time), might criticize the length of the season as compared with Lent and Passion-Tide; but in this case they must also criticize the Gospels, which have the same proportion, thus making clear from the first that the Church considered the Passion of the Lord as of chief importance to believers. It is of course true, however, that these six Sundays, several of which are often missed out, are quite inadequate to give in any fullness the account of the Ministry. The method is purely suggestive, and the principle of selection will grow clear as we proceed.

In the week of Epiphany I, we remember the silent years at Nazareth. The Epistle, with its call to present our bodies a living sacrifice, is a fitting prelude to the contemplation of those years, in which thought loves to dwell upon the Workman Christ, the child and lad in Joseph's shop, earning bread by daily labor. Art and letters have combined to add vividness to the lovely scene, a scene surely authentic as is proved by one precious phrase in St. Mark's story: "Is not this the Carpenter?"

The drama of the Gospels has as its setting the world of homely and normal toil. The pastoral life, at the outset, is shown in easy commerce with angelic hosts; agricultural and domestic life is the background of most of the Master's parables. One can not help feeling that certain occupations bring Him especially near: the doctor and the teacher can claim Him in special sense as head of the profession. But the trade of building, with its sacred task of sheltering humanity, is most closely of all consecrated by His direct labor:

"In the shop of Nazareth
    Pungent cedar haunts the breath.

"In the room the Craftsman stands,—
Stands and reaches out His Hands. . .
Let the shadow veil His Face
If you must, and dimly trace
His workman's tunic, girt with bands
At the waist. But the Hands,—
Let the light play on them,
Marks of toil lay on them.

"When night comes, and I turn
From my shop, where I earn
Daily bread, let me see
Those hard Hands, know that He
Shared my lot every bit,
Was a man every whit.

"Carpenter, hard like Thine
Is this hand,—this of mine,—
I reach out, gripping Thee,
Son of Man, close to me,
Close and fast, fearlessly."[1]

The Gospel for the day leads us behind those
years of toil to the Holy Childhood, and in the
divine anecdote of Christ among the doctors gives
an unforgettably significant picture. The intellectual eagerness of the Child strikes one first; for
surely Jesus, listening to the learned men and

[1] Arthur Vaughan: Hands of Toil.

questioning them, was not consciously their teacher, laying down the law with painful precocity, as a false art suggests; He was the little learner, swift of understanding, marvellously docile and wise. His intense absorption, oblivious of His family, is a completely human touch: "How is it that ye sought me?" Of course I should be here! To say with Blake that the Lord "scorned earth's parents" is surely wrong; yet throughout the Gospels ("Who is my mother and my brethren?") there is a gentle uncompromising subordination of personal claims, however intimate, to supreme purpose, which may be well if cautiously applied to certain not infrequent modern perplexities. None the less, the story ends with the welcome statement of His subjection: "Subject to them,"—to Joseph as well as to Mary. Of Joseph we really know one fact only, apart from his trade: he was a "just man," and it is not over-fantastic to think of Justice as the foster-father, while Love is the mother, of the Lord on earth.

During the five remaining Sundays of the season, the thought of Manifestation follows a double line, lightly indicated owing to necessary compression, but full of interest. The Epistles dwell on the progressive manifestation of the Christian law of love in that fellowship of light, the Christian Church. It is a Church not yet run into ecclesiastical grooves, but a Beloved Community, bent upon its great and amazing adventure of revealing to the world for the first time the supernatural work of grace. All the passages till the last are from the noble pioneer St. Paul; I to V consecutively from Romans XII and XIII, V from Colossians; and the climacteric Epistle from the sixth Sunday is from St. John. And while the Epistles are developing the principles of Christian ethics as discovered in the Mystical Body, and registering informally the creation of an entirely new type of character, the Gospels present the Prototype of all Christian men. They dwell on Christ's ministry, in its dual aspect of deeds and words; the first three Epiphany Sundays presenting examples of His miracles, the last two of His teaching.

Let us study the Epistles first; they are really a sort of running commentary, developing in the normal and social life of the group the qualities which the Gospels imply. And it is astonishing how much Gospel teaching St. Paul can crowd into a few lines.

The key-note has been struck in the first Sunday: it is no less than a transformation of the natural man: "Be ye not conformed to this

world,"—or as the Revised Version has it, "fashioned according,"—"but be ye transformed in the
renewal of your mind." We proceed to see what
is involved in that transformation and renewal.
Paul is nothing if not practical. Take the frank,
straight-from-the-shoulder instruction of the passage for the second Sunday: Concentrate your
attention on what you are competent to do, since
gifts differ. Give simply,—instinctively, liberally,—manage efficiently if that is your business,
be cheerful in your social service and philanthropy, candid about your loving. Loathe evil
things, stick to the good. Don't be captious or
critical, but good-natured, affectionate and fraternal, putting other people ahead of yourself in
esteem (did the apostle include trade-relations in
this precept?). Energy is repeatedly stressed;
laziness in secular affairs is no Christian trait;
but fervor in spirit must go with vigor in action.
Serve the Lord: be able to rejoice in hope rather
than in fulfilment ("What I aspired to be, and
was not, comforts me"); and be patient in the
troubles that are sure to come. Pray insistently.
Share your possessions, but with discrimination.
Be systematically hospitable. See the point of
view of those who are unpleasant to you; wish
them well, don't get impatient with them, the
apostle repeats anxiously, knowing that he asks

a hard thing. Be really sympathetic, glad with the glad as well as sorry with the sorrowing. Don't be moody, but equable, and find the basis of agreement with one another. Don't pay attention to "high things," worldly rank or honor, get down to the level with plain people, men of low estate. The injunctions tumble out as fast as the pen of the apostle can form them; one feels that he writes in joyous elation. A new beauty, the beauty of homely practical holiness, revealed in fellowship, is dawning on the world. Christian character is becoming defined; and the whole Ser mon on the Mount is in solution in the passage.

No, not the whole; for the next two Epistles carry on the theme. The third Epistle, direct commentary it would seem on Christ's own words, treats that most difficult of Christian duties, the right attitude toward enemies. It might literally be called "Above the Battle-field " Some virtues can be dismissed with a succinct effective phrase; not this, which so contradicts nature that Paul himself has to modify his injunction with an anxious: "If it be possible,—as much as lieth in you,—live peaceably." But despite modifications, he gives a singularly direct transcript of one of the Master's most emphasized and violated commands.

How violated on a national scale, it is needless

if not seditious to indicate; there is more edifica-
tion in noting instances even in the midst of war,
of obedience to it,—that of the soldier who
tramped two hours to secure his ration, only to
give it to the hungry prisoner at his side; that
of the woman who served hot cocoa to the tired
soldiers who had just burned her little home, with
the result that when ordered to burn the next village the men refused and were shot in conse-
quence,—doubtless to their eternal gain. Thank
God, Christian people have often behaved in this
way; but instances of similar national policy are
far to seek. The excellent outcome of England's
policy to the Boers and of our return of the Boxer
indemnity gave hints, which no nation of late
seems inclined to follow. If thine enemy hunger,
feed him, is a precept which men have been forced
to obey by the cruel logic of events to recognize
as necessary and sensible; but how reluctantly
they were forced, and how bitter to thoughtful
people the absence in this fearsome post-war
period, of magnanimous impulses toward a conquered foe!

Lest the implication of Paul's teaching seem
a little revolutionary perhaps, the fourth Epistle
is the apostle at his most conservative, and that
is very conservative indeed. Not for nothing was

he a Roman citizen and proud of the fact! It is
an extremely non-resistant passage, which taken
literally would make the changes now in process
in the world-order quite impossible; and it makes
a curious prelude to a mighty and disturbing
Gospel. Yet the idea of a mystic power, inherent
in authorities once constituted, calling for loyalty till those authorities are changed, may be
construed in a way not inconsistent with consti-
tutional democracy; indeed the only "powers that
be" which the modern man easily recognizes as
"ordained of God" are democratic powers.
Paul's practical mind is free from any illusions
about human nature even when men are trying to
be Christian. Earnestly he reiterates in the
lovely passage from Colossians which is the fifth
Epistle, that same old need for "humbleness of
mind,"—for meekness, long-suffering, forbear-
ance: that "mutual forgiveness of each vice"
which Blake calls "The gates of Paradise."
Only love, which is "the bond of perfectness" can
establish men in these virtues. But love can do
all things; it can create the spiritual unity which
is divine peace and unfading joy. These Pauline
passages end their exposition of "the fellowship
of the Mystery" on the note of lyric rapture—the
blessed Society of those in Christ singing with

grace in their hearts to the Lord, and in all they do in word and deed giving thanks to the Father in the Name of the Lord Jesus.

The very beauty of this picture of the Christian society as it unfolds carries for us implicit rebuke. In a civilization where anxious self-protection is a necessary duty, and the defensive attitude, whether in trade or in national politics, becomes the recognized expression of loyalty and patriotism, it is impossible to realize the full power of the apostolic ideal. That ideal is charged with mysterious force; whenever it gets a chance, in private lives, where it is less handicapped than in social applications, it is a continuous Epiphany, a revelation of heavenly attraction. But only in proportion as Christianity creates an environment in which this free liberal and joyous life of brotherhood can be realized without restraint, will it continue to manifest the Lord of Glory.

If such thoughts are sobering, the last Epiphany Epistle brings comfort and reassurance, for it is full of hope.[1] It turns from Paul to John, and its assertion that we are now, despite our weakness, the sons of God, prefaces the exultant

[1] It is ordered that when there are fewer than six Sundays after Epiphany, this Epistle and Gospel shall be used at the end of the Trinity Season; and in fact they are so used more often than not. They are as appropriate to introduce Advent as to end Epiphany.

addition: "It doth not yet appear what we shall be; but we know that when He shall appear we shall be like Him, for we shall see Him as He is." Thus shall manifestation, begun on earth, be perfected in a triumphant eternity. None the less, John the mystic is no less practical, no less severe, than Paul the moralist. "Let no man deceive you; he that doeth righteousness is righteous; he that committeth sin is of the devil." "Sin!" It has not before been explicitly mentioned in the Epiphany Scriptures; here at the end of the season, it is suddenly, sharply stressed.

For the consummation of Epiphany, the ultimate purpose for which "The Son of God was manifested," is just here, as St. John says: that He might "take away our sins," might "destroy the works of the Devil." This is a victory which only the Sinless can achieve; and the Sinlessness of Christ is His final self-revelation. To be made like unto Him,—to purify ourselves even as He is pure,—this is the summit of our desire; this would be an Epiphany indeed.

From the beginning of the season, the Gospels, to the study of which we now return, show phases of the Sinless Life. The Epistles deal with an ethic which would have no point in solitude but could only be developed in a Beloved Community.

In like manner, the Gospels are social, showing the Lord in His relations with His brethren.

Many of the traits given in the second Epistle are stressed in the Gospel for that day: the Miracle at Cana. The Master, glad with the glad at that marriage feast, kindly affectioned toward wedding guests and perturbed host, ministers to their necessity, giving simply and liberally, and is Himself the hospitable host as He manifests His glory by that generous act of turning water into wine which He still stands ready to perform at every feast where He may be invoked. The miracle,—exalted by the Greek Church into a special post of honor,—is the solemn consecration of marriage and so of all normal human ties. This is the first of the mighty deeds selected by the Church for our instruction. It shows the Lord in relation to a world pure and happy, though needing the Giver of all good to sustain its joy, and it shuts out decisively all false asceticism and sets the Sacramental seal on social life.

In the third Epiphany Gospel, on the other hand, Christ is shown in a world at enmity with itself, diseased in body and soul. The double healing of the leper and of the Centurion's servant, suggests a wide range of social service; for leprosy and palsy are types respectively of un-

cleanness and helplessness, and the primal aims
of the servant of the community must always be
to cleanse and invigorate the body politic, as well
as the bodies of individuals in need. Swiftly,
instantly, comes the Divine Help; not grudgingly,
with "organized charity scrimped and iced," but
in response to the first word of desire.

In the Gospel for the fourth Sunday, the
"mighty works" of the Lord mount into a more
mystical and difficult region: power over the
forces of nature is shown in the stilling of the
storm, power over the mysterious world of spiritual evil in the exorcism of the Gadarene devils.
It is noteworthy that the control of nature, which
man can so far attain only indirectly, by progressive mastery of science, comes with apparent ease
to the harmonious manhood of the Lord; the second of these two miracles appears to be by far
the most difficult and costly.

The Scriptures appointed for these three Sundays have been marked by joy in the varied manifestations of the Divine Glory. Yet there is a
stern undercurrent. The faith which can alone
release that manifestation is all too rare. "I have
not found so great faith, no not in Israel," says
Jesus in sad surprise of the Roman centurion;
and He continues with mingled exaltation and

sorrow to tell of the many who shall come from east and west and north and south, to sit at the Feast while the children of the kingdom shall be cast into outer darkness. The idea of a Chosen Nation has today been supplanted by that of a Chosen Church, and the children of the kingdom are, one fears, the respectable members of it: shall the sorrow of the Lord be repeated again?

"O ye of little faith," is again the reproach to the frightened disciples on the tossing lake. But the climax of faithlessness is found in the miracle among the Gadarenes, which contains one of the most terrible texts in the New Testament. When the miracle was completed, "the whole city came out to meet Jesus; and when they saw Him they besought Him that He would depart out of their coasts." . . . Why this awful desire? Because, in emancipating a human soul, property had perished! Some people are much concerned about those pigs which were drowned in the lake, and the story certainly presents difficulties. But one point is clear,—the mistake made by the inhabitants of Gadara. They all came out to meet Him who had set their fellows free from a fate of inconceivable horror. But they had no joy in that deliverance, they felt no gratitude. They begged Him to depart, as a nuisance, for they preferred to keep both their pigs and their demoniacs.

"Rabbi, begone! Thy powers
Bring loss to us and ours.
Our ways are not as Thine,—
Thou lovest men, we—swine.
O get you hence, Omnipotence,
And take this fool of Thine!
His soul? What care we for his soul?
What good to us that Thou hast made him whole,
Since we have lost our swine!"[1]

As Epiphany II, III and IV show the Master as
Man of Action, Epiphany V and VI show Him as
Teacher. Perhaps because the more usual and
ethical elements in His teaching have been suf-
ficiently suggested in the preceding Epistles, these
Gospels both emphasize once more the Apocalyptic outlook. The parable of the Tares instills the
need for toleration in view of judgment at the
coming harvest, and the great Coming is as explicitly predicted as in any Advent Scripture, in
the passage from St. Matthew for the last
Epiphany Sunday.[2] It is striking to observe that
the Church never allows us to rest in the present:
when all is serenest in the progressive manifestation of the Divine Life, she sounds once more
the note of prescient dread and hope.

[1] John Oxenham.
[2] See Note, p. 78.

The first Epiphany Collect was a prayer for knowledge· "That we, who know Thee now by faith, may after this life have the fruition of Thy glorious Godhead" The last, echoing the Epistle, is a prayer for holiness· "That having this hope we may purify ourselves, even as He is pure."

So does Epiphany lead out toward Lent, Manifestation toward Penitence. An undercurrent of sadness, a growing sense of shame, may be clearly discerned throughout the joyous weeks. None the less, the prevalent temper of this season is praise and glad thanksgiving. Christianity, new-born, faces the task of expansion rather than of repentance. Thought is centred not in ourselves, but in the Sinless Master, Who albeit He moves through a bewildered and latently hostile world, proceeds with serene and gracious joy on His great work of instruction and healing. It is, like Advent, a season of flux, of hope; the exhilaration attendant on discovery and growth pervades and suffuses it. There could be no better summary of its spirit than that given in the last year of his life by the great social Christian, Scott Holland:

"Epiphany is both the salute and the call to adventure. It is the summons to dare the illimitable tracts of the desert for one remote and intangible star. . . . The promise, it may be, is never the promise we look for. Abraham looked for a whole land and found only a grave: the children of Abraham looked for rest and found unrest: the wise men set forth for a king and found a child: the twelve sought for a prince and discovered a Cross. It is ever so. To none is the promise ever fulfilled. Not here. But no matter. The one vital need is to go on,—after the gleam. Adventurers all!

"Then the adventure itself. What is that? Well, it is surely the very living of the life,—His Life. To be that, to live that,—that is the soul of the Christian endeavour. Within the short earthly life there is always the temper of adventure. It begins in boyhood among the Temple doctors. He casts Himself adrift: He disappears: He is lost. So again in the later years. . . . He has no home: no regular and ordered routine: no set hours: no guarded and secluded times for rest and meat. No! He just "goes about": He wanders at random: He depends upon charity. Then, as He adventures Himself, so He calls upon others to take risks too. Launch out: sell all: forsake everything, 'Follow Me.'

"And it is Epiphany that recalls to us this essential note of our common creed. . . . Yet it is a little odd to see how quick we are to admire the touch of adventure in others while we rather back from it for ourselves. We all read "lives" of St. Francis, but it hardly seems to dawn upon us that the spirit of St. Francis is but the unrestrained expression of a mood that should be strong in every believing heart   It is probably the feeling that he was right that has been the secret of the undying inspiration of his name through the centuries.

". . . Shall then the Epiphany challenge go unanswered and unheard? Will no one take it up? Shall the spirit that stirs today in a thousand thousand soldier souls find no counterpart in the Christian heart and in the life of the Church at home? If only it could! If only here and there men would break away from the ordinary ways, and do big and bold and rash deeds in the name and for the sake of Him Who made Himself of no reputation and took upon Him the form of a servant, what might not happen, what might not come to pass?"[1]

[1] Scott Holland in *The Commonwealth*, Epiphany, 1918.

CHAPTER IV: SEPTUAGESIMA TO LENT

Antiphon: I so run, not as uncertainly;
so fight I, not as one that beateth the air.
V. Though I bestow all my goods to feed
the poor, and have not charity,
R. It profiteth me nothing.

O Lord, Who hast taught us that all our
doings without charity are nothing worth;
Send Thy Holy Ghost, and pour into our
hearts that most excellent gift of charity,
the very bond of peace and of all virtues,
without which whosoever liveth is counted
dead before Thee. Grant this for Thine
only Son Jesus Christ's sake. Amen.

CHAPTER IV: SEPTUAGESIMA TO LENT

"Alleluia can not always
Be our song while here below."

ALREADY the later Epiphany Sundays have
hinted at new aspects of the faith. Throughout the season, we have watched manifestation
widen, as Truth like light irradiates the world.
But that world is set even in the hearts of the disciples. Christianity as interpreted by mortals is
no transparent medium for transmitting the divine
light. It must itself be cleansed, and as we pursue
the adventure of discovering its power and meaning, the sense of inadequacy brings increasing sadness. A craving awakens in the soul which re-
quires a new emphasis. In three interesting Sundays, with names which, though colorless in themselves, count forward through the shadows to the
Easter dawn, the transition to new experience is
accomplished.

Septuagesima strikes the frank note of confession in the prayer, from the Sarum missal,
"that we who are justly punished for our offences

89

3 weeks
Voluntary fasting
in prep for
fasting.
required

may be mercifully delivered by Thy goodness, for the glory of Thy Name." The invigorating Epistle is an incentive to energy in the race, and a warning lest those who have sought to manifest the light should themselves be cast into darkness; the missionary zeal of Epiphany is thus called to a temporary halt, and deepened by the stern summons to self-discipline and introspection. The Gospel is the parable of the Laborers in the Vineyard, or, as it is sometimes called, of the Eleventh Hour.

If people are candid, they usually confess that this story outrages their sense of justice. "These last have worked but one hour, and thou hast made them equal unto us, which have borne the burden and heat of the day." An arbitrary performance, contradicting our ideas of what is suitable, and our most accredited economic principles.

John Ruskin was fully alive to the contradiction; therefore, he chose the words of the householder, "Friend, I do thee no wrong. . . . I will give *unto this last* even as unto thee," for the title of his most challenging book. The book challenges us still, though its root-principle, that reward be measured less by productive values than by the worker's readiness and need, is not so startling today as in 1860. At that date, the idea that inequity might result from free competition, and that the habit of taking advantage of a glut in the labor-market to buy labor cheap might have been discountenanced by Jesus, was shocking to the British public. Ruskin's friend Thackeray had to suppress the chapters of the book, which were running through his magazine, *The Cornhill.* Today, this idea, though still distasteful in many quarters, has become familiar; and we are in a better position than our fathers to realize the implications of the story.

Now a parable is not a treatise on industrial life; and any economic inference from Our Lord's words is sure to be criticized by many people who always wish to confine His meaning to what they call the "spiritual" sphere,—by which they usually mean the personal. And undoubtedly the spiritual and personal application is paramount and permanent. The feeble, the frustrated, the baffled, who long in vain for permission to gather the grapes of the Lord and to press them into wine which shall make glad the heart of man, —all people neglected or impotent in the mystic vineyard of interior experience, or on more practical planes, can take heart of grace from the story. They too, at the eleventh hour, shall be sent forth to labor, and shall be judged worthy of the full reward; for the Law of the Spirit does not measure values by earthly measurements, and

often numbers among the most creative and productive, those who only stand and wait.

But it is dangerous to avoid applying Christian principles to social and industrial life, by
relegating them to a purely "spiritual" sphere.
That time-honored evasion contradicts the whole
Sacramental philosophy. The very point of the
great truths radiating from the Incarnation, is
that one harmonious law runs through all spheres
of being, wherever the Grace of God controls the
world; and since our business is to regulate earthly
dealings by this divine law, we have no right to
deny economic significance to this parable.

That significance lies quite plainly on the surface. These are the Unemployed who stand all
day in the market place, because no man has hired
them; and the "penny a day," for which the
workmen have contracted, represents, as Ruskin
saw, a sort of "National Minimum," or living
wage; for the "penny" in Biblical times was regarded as a fair average wage for a day's work.
The obvious moral is, that society should not de-
prive men of this wage when they are idle through
no fault of their own.

This is a good trade-union parable; indeed, it
seems to go a little further than normal trade-
union practise, and to suggest the Saint-Simonian
formula, which today so powerfully controls great

sections of the proletarian mind: "From each according to his capacity; to each according to his needs." It is a formula which might carry us far, conceivably toward a Soviet system. It is hardly an exaggeration to say that all schemes for social reconstruction are implicit in it. And to find this clear if paradoxical exposition of divine justice at the turn to the season of penitence, is certainly suggestive. Just in proportion as civilization grows toward this justice, it will reject the idea, so native to the natural man, that disparity of reward is a necessary incentive to labor, and will refuse to listen when workers or anyone else grumble over equality. For in its treatment of people it will look less to their achievement than to their necessities and less to their past than to their future. It will be placed on the sure foundation of supplying to every man, not what he has earned, but what will best enable him to develop a richer manhood.

The sentence, "Is it not lawful for me to do what I will with my own?" is difficult. It seems to recognize an arbitrary standard of property, and the difficulty is not solved by the fact that the Goodman is the Lord. One can at least say that the parable, realistic like all Christ's illustrations, takes the world as it is, and that if all employers used authority over "their own" for this sort of decision, private ownership would be less challenged than it is now. The closing words, ''For the last shall be first and the first shall be last,'' are said not to have formed part of the original story, to which indeed they seem slightly irrelevant. But even if spoken on another occasion, they form an integral part of Christ's teaching. When shall we begin to express the principle they imply, in the economic structure?

The Greek Church uses for the Gospel of this Sunday the parable of the Prodigal; and the lesson of the two parables is much the same. Both score the jealousy of the self-righteous, which has so very real a case in the eyes of the world. People who sympathize with the grumbling laborers will sympathize with the grumbling Elder Brother. These were all excellent persons, faithful and dutiful workmen. They judged according to the world's judgment, on which existing society is erected as on a stable and just foundation. But they were not perfected in love, and therefore they could not recognize the higher justice, which is not primarily concerned with deserts or services but with needs and possibilities. Love rejoices that the prodigal rather than the dutiful son should have the fatted calf. Love is glad to see the idle, the weak, the rejected, admitted to an equality with the strong, the energetic, the successful.

"Faith will vanish into sight;
 Hope be emptied in delight;
 Love in Heaven will shine more bright,
  Therefore, give us love."

The note of Sexagesima is the note of Christian heroism. The superb enumeration of his trials by the apostle should put our smooth lives to shame, and quicken in us the craving for Lenten discipline. It is not surprising that the Greek Church makes in this week a special commemoration of ascetics. Lives may not always be smooth; we are particularly aware of that fact in these anxious times, when Fear hovers over the world like a bird of prey. But the Christian must be ready at any moment to welcome opportunities for perils, weariness and painfulness, for watch ings, hunger and thirst, cold and nakedness. The social revolution may quite conceivably call for all these forms of Christian witnessing.

In the Gospel and in other devotions of the week, the Greek Church again emphasizes the judgment to come. But our Anglican Gospel is the parable of the Sower. This, like the other parable just studied, reveals an eternal principle which should receive not only a personal but a social application. For the natural picture is suggested of a community with varying social conditions. The thin and sterile soil in which the good seed can with difficulty mature, will be recognized by every social worker as an apt image for the poverty in which all better ideals and interests, however sedulously implanted, are prone to wither. The other type of ground, in which the thorny cares and pleasures and riches of this life stifle the little plants of holiness, is one in which all too many of us are trying to grow our souls. "The cares of this world and the deceitfulness of riches," is the description in St. Matthew; and the apposite phrases have that exact felicity often possessed by the words of Him Who was master of language as well as of men's hearts. They describe accurately two evils of which He stands in constant dread: the cares, from which men continually create a false standard of duty, so that they are tethered as it were to anxious thought for the morrow; the deceitfulness, which is the most subtle characteristic of wealth, and which explains why the Lord habitually deprecated and feared riches for His followers.

Jesus is intensely anxious that His disciples shall catch the full force of this parable. "He

cried and said, He that hath ears to hear let him
hear,'' is one of the living touches assuring us
that we listen to an authentic tradition.

These, so He tells the more intimate group that
questions Him, are the mysteries of the Kingdom
of God. The Church from the opening of Advent
has directed our attention repeatedly to that
Kingdom as a future ideal, connected with a
cataclysmic end of the age. At this point, as in
Epiphany V and in Septuagesima, she invites us
to dwell upon it as a principle of normal and secret growth; the fullness of the Master's thought
can only be compassed by inclusion of both ideas,
for both are necessary clues to the true interpretation of history. And when we recall the funda-
mentally social meaning inherent in the conception of the Kingdom to every faithful Jew, we are
reinforced in our conviction that these parables
all assuredly apply not only to inward disposi-
tion but to outward circumstance. Seed is not
ours to create; it is given us by a perpetual
miracle. But it is ours to plant and the preparation of the soil is distinctly our business. All
programmes of social welfare are a matter either
of preparing the soil or of planting the seed.

On Quinquagesima Sunday, Lent is close; and
beautiful introduction is given to the season of

penitence, by the great exaltation of love. The Reformation Collect, composed in 1549, is in perfect unison with the Epistle and Gospel, which are the same as in the Sarum missal, the manuscript missal of Leofric, and the ancient Lectionary of the Roman Church. In the Greek Church, the story of the Fall is recounted on this Sunday; our custom is more tender.

On the social character of St. Paul's great love-lyric it is surely needless to dwell. With superb and convincing ease it sweeps away the achievements of the orator, the scholar, the fanatic, the philanthropist, yes, of the martyr, as in themselves of no avail. The burning passion of the man who feared lest when he had preached to others he might himself become a castaway, his stern avoidance of self-deception, speak through every line. The enumeration of the ''notes'' of love is wholly practical; it could have been written only by a man of the world, moving among his fellow men. It was St. Teresa, most exalted of cloistered mystics, who said cannily that we could only be sure that we loved God by watching ourselves to see if we loved our brothers; and St. Paul is here wholly concerned with the test of love by the plain human behavior to other people. If we are kind and patient and modest, if we are free from envy and soreness, if we instinctively shrink from a critical interpretation, and hate to know about badness, instead of gloating over it as some "good people" do, if we can bear all things, believe all things, hope all things, endure all things,—why then we have our share in the love that never fails, and have escaped from the temporal order into the eternal. Now we see reality only darkly, reflected as in a mirror; but some day we are to see face to Face, and know even as we are known. That perfect knowledge, says the apostle, shall be perfect love: an assertion of Christian faith, putting to rout the insidious fears of the cynic.

It is well that this meditation on true charity should precede our summons to the stern self-disciplines of Lent: lest as we seek the higher sanctities, the mood of the Pharisee should betray us and we turn hard. There are three types of people: the first, including most of us, whose standards for others are more severe than those for themselves: the second, who have a high standard for personal life but insist on a like standard for others: and finally the third and Christian type, which St. Paul wishes to recommend,—severe toward itself, lenient toward its brethren. As a man mounts to the higher levels in his quest of sanctity, the second type is that to avoid.

The Quinquagesima Gospel has, as is fitting, the first, solemn prediction of the Passion; and the prayer of blind Bartimæus, "Lord, that I may receive my sight," is the cry of the soul, born out of all the teaching which precedes.

CHAPTER V · THE SEASON OF LENT

Antiphon: As sorrowful, yet always rejoicing; as poor, yet making many rich; as having nothing, and yet possessing all things.

V. Sanctify a fast, call a solemn assembly;

R. Gather the people, sanctify the congregation.

O Lord, Who for our sakes didst fast forty days and forty nights; Give us grace to use such abstinence, that, our flesh being subdued to the Spirit, we may ever obey Thy godly motions in righteousness, and true holiness, to Thy honour and glory, Who livest and reignest with the Father and the Holy Ghost, one God, world without end. Amen.

EPIPHANY leads the gaze outward to the spread of the Good News through the world; Lent leads it inward, Easter upward. To watch and share the expansion of the Gospel of the Kingdom was at first pure joy. But Christianity undefiled, illumining a hostile world, is not the whole story. The three Sundays of transition have changed our mood. Progressive vision normally ends in humility and shame; now, only the ashes on the brow can satisfy the penitent soul.

The Church grew slowly into recognizing the necessity for Lent, and the present length of the season is arbitrary. "It seems clear that the original fast before Easter was one of forty hours, this being the period between the death of Our Lord and His resurrection."[1] Gradually and irregularly the time was extended; Ash-Wednesday, and the three days preceding the first Lenten Sunday were probably added by Gregory the Great. The present length of the season, though

[1] The Prayer-Book Interleaved. Campion and Beamont, p. 99.

103

not primitive, was apparently determined by the fifth century.

It has been challenged lately. The charge is made that Lent has become formal, marked chiefly by the multiplication of services which over-work the clergy and bore the congregation; that nobody should be called to repent his sins six weeks on end; and that a shortened period, say a fortnight, might possibly be used in an intensive way, as a time of real and fresh contrition.

There is no historical or psychological sanc-tion for any special number of weeks, and the point is worth considering. But it is strange to choose this special epoch of world-story in which to say that Christians dedicate too much time to penitence! Rather might it well be claimed that our year just now should be a perpetual Lent, at-tuned to the cry of Bartimæus: May the Lord open our eyes, and grant our shamed repentance power to restore justice among the nations of men!

It is to be noted, moreover, that the present ordering of the season does not call for six weeks of steady introspection and self-castigation. Dur-ing four weeks, the faithful recognize the stern assaults of evil, and abide in the wilderness with their Lord; during the last two, even while the Fast endures, they turn with softened hearts to the Vision of Salvation. And even so, the case is stated too strongly, for the fourth Sunday in Lent, to which the tender names of Refreshment Sunday or Mothering Sunday have been given, is charged with exquisite consolation.

These thoughts, however, may be considered evasions of the issue. For it must frankly be confessed that penitence even in small doses has become unpopular. Whole systems of religion decry it as morbid, and bid us relegate it to the lumber-house of obsolete spiritual oppressions, while in endless monotony we "hold the thought" of health and joy and stereotype our smile. Almost everybody is infected with uneasy impatience against self-examination. Look out, not in, and lend a hand; in other words, take up social service and work energetically for others without bothering about yourself: that is the modern counsel.

Such precepts are a reaction from very genuine overstrain which the middle-aged can remember. Yet Catholic thought, always on guard against excess from any side, can not accept them. To that thought, sin is grimmest reality, to be met not by evasion or denial, but in conscious fight, desperate as ever Christian waged with Apollyon.

Dean Inge, in a suggestive little book on *Types*

of Christian Saintliness, claims that the idea of holiness is characteristically Catholic. "The Catholic saint," says he, "has a horror of sin and a shrinking from it which the Protestant would think morbid." Protestant virtue on the other hand centres to him in a sense of direct inward inspiration leading to intense individualism; while the Liberal Christian, whom he treats as a third type more common nowadays, has for his vital centre the pure passion for truth. Dean Inge quotes with agreement a remark of Sir Oliver Lodge, that "the modern man is not worrying over his sins at all," and he says plainly· "I should regard this defective sense of sin as the chief flaw" in the liberal type of Christian.

Generalizations are always insecure. One can not forget the intense and passionate remorse of the old Puritans, as shown in a book like Bunyan's *Grace Abounding;* and that very overstrain spoken of above was the result of the unwholesome lengths to which introspection was carried in early New England. As for inward inspiration, Dean Inge has a hard time of it to get around the Catholic mystics, who certainly specialized as much as Protestants on that line. But if the Catholic tradition does in the long run place more steady stress than Protestant or Liberal on human sinfulness, that tradition should be revived; for it is rooted deep in reality. Any honest man, as he watches his poor consciousness, poisoned by prejudices and distastes, bound by earthiness, inhibited by egotisms, has a right to cry out in anguish: "An enemy has done this." He should pay alert attention to that enemy. He should watch its manœuvres, he should trace it to its hidden lair, and there he should fight it to the death. In last analysis, the war against evil must be fought out on the battle-ground of personality.

But not on that battle-ground alone; and one important way to escape unreality or morbidness in our contrition and to restore the fading sense of sin, is to supplement personal self-examination and penitence by resolute social shame.

In this way, we may unite what is best in the Catholic, Protestant, and Liberal tradition: the deep horror of sin which marks the Catholic, with the active conflict against it which Dean Inge says marks the evangelical Protestant, and the keen interest in a better world which we all recognize as characteristic of the Liberal Christian. And we shall assuredly be following the method

of Christ. For the Lord's dealing with evil is full
of a sane objectivity, as is also that of His Church.

There is no experience so private as penitence;
there is no season so social as Lent. From the
very outset, the fact is clear. The first impulse
of a man when he is ashamed of himself is to run
away and hide; but Lent has no indulgence for
that impulse. "Blow the trumpet in Zion, call a
solemn assembly: gather the people, sanctify the
congregation, assemble the elders, gather the
children, and those that suck the breasts: let the
bridegroom go forth of his chamber, and the bride
out of her closet. Let the priests, the ministers
of the Lord, weep between the porch and the altar,
and let them say, Spare thy people, O Lord, and
give not thine heritage to reproach." . . . The
publicity is actually ceremonial; it is fearful in
its solemnity. The first sense of sin to be engen-
dered is the corporate, the national sense. Israel
is to repent as one man and the recognition of
this necessity pervades the Old Testament at its
deepest. Even when the note is poignantly personal, as sometimes, for instance, in the Penitential Psalms, there is the turn at the end: "Out
of the depths have I called unto Thee, O Lord.
. . . O Israel trust in the Lord." . . . "Have

mercy upon me, O Lord. . . . Wash me thoroughly from my wickedness." . . . But then instantly· "O be favorable and gracious unto Zion, build Thou the walls of Jerusalem."

Study of the Lenten Scriptures in their entirety brings out with startling force the intention of the Church that personal penitence shall be rooted in the sense of national contrition. How impressive they are,—these passages from the Old Testament, which reach us across the abyss of the generations with accent clear as that of yesterday!

"Thus saith the Lord of Hosts: . . . If ye thoroughly amend your ways and your doings, if ye thoroughly execute justice between a man and his neighbor, if ye oppress not the stranger" (how about the alien enemy?), "the fatherless and the widow, and shed not innocent blood in this place then will I cause you to dwell in this place in the land which I gave to your fathers, forever and ever. Behold ye trust in lying words that can not profit. . . . Is this house which is called by my name become a den of robbers in your eyes? Behold, even I have seen it, saith the Lord." [1]

"Son of man, when the land sinneth against me by trespassing grievously, then will I stretch out mine hand upon it and will break the staff

[1] Jeremiah vii, 1-11.

of the bread thereof and will send famine upon it and will cut off man and beast from it."[1]

"Show My people their transgression, and the house of Jacob their sins   Behold in the day of your fast ye find pleasure and exact all your labors. Behold ye fast for strife and debate and to smite with the fist of wickedness.   Is not this the fast that I have chosen? To loose the bands of wickedness, to undo the heavy burdens, and to let the oppressed go free, and that ye break every yoke? Is it not to deal thy bread to the hungry and that thou bring the poor that are cast out to thy house? When thou seest the naked that thou cover him; and that thou hide not thyself from thine own flesh?"[2]

This last great phrase in particular never fails, when Ash-Wednesday comes round, to thrill and appal with its tragic modernity. That thou hide not thyself from thine own flesh! How accurately it describes our worst offence, penetrating to the centre of our sin and shame,—our class-exclusiveness, our group-provincialism, our national arrogance and jealous instinct of self-protection! The sins are social, the penitence must be social, and social must the expiation be.

"The first thing to do is to pray sensibly and

[1] Ezekiel xiv, 13.
[2] Isaiah lviii, 1-7. All these passages are from the Lenten Lessons.

deeply .. that the diabolic spirit of war, whether it manifests itself in the ghastly convulsion of shot and shell, or whether, vampire-like, it slowly drains the life-blood of a nation by its bitter class-jealousy, its materialism, its mammon-worship, may be forever banished from our lives."[1]

Perhaps the sense of sin which was fast becoming unreal to our stalwart and shallow generation could be renewed by nothing short of some great shock, forcing men to face a world delivered over to terror by the results of their own blindness and wrong-doing. That shock came in 1914, and it is not expended yet. As revolution succeeds war, and the struggle between classes throws even the titanic anguish of four momentous years into the shadow, thoughtful men experience more and more completely a consciousness of guilty responsibility for the causes of world catastrophe. It becomes apparent that no shifting of blame nor concentration of it on one source is possible. The crimes of every nation, not least our own, lie upon us with a bitter weight: imperialistic ambition and commercial greed, sullen class-antagonisms, lowering suspi-

[1] Rev. E. M. Venables.

cions, tortuous cruelties to those without, grasping meanness toward those within.

Most of us have had no immediate concern with these evils as individuals; indeed, to a large extent, the wrong inheres in a system which is an unconscious growth and for which no one, not the capitalist nor the politician, nor any one else, is directly responsible today. Men have been blinder than Bartimæus, but as we of the democratic nations receive our sight, with what terrible clearness loom before us our irresponsibility, our lazy acquiescence in racial and class antagonisms, our impossible economic conditions, our national policies, sure to ripen into disaster! Sins, negligences, ignorances,—only confession can heal us,—confession, and such reparation as can be made by a reconstruction of society from its very base, in its international and industrial relationships. Shallow men may plume themselves on seeing red, and acquire cheap merit by invective against the sins of Germany or of the Bolsheviks. That is emphatically a method closed to the Christian. Israel had enemies enough; but the prophets did not keep busy denouncing the sins of Assyria, nor did they enjoin such denunciations as a duty on the people of Jehovah.

Israel, in the Old Testament, is not only nation but Church. The sorrowful rebukes of the Lord are addressed to His Chosen People, who should be His witnesses on earth yet have turned themselves to idols. How about the modern Church? Divided, piteous, inept, its failure to afford leadership toward social righteousness scandalizes the non-Christian world. Through vast portions of nominal Christendom, the forces which aim to restore their heritage to the meek, encounter not only passivity but fierce opposition on the part of organized religion. Among us Anglo-Saxons, the situation is less clear-cut. Religion, though hesitant and backward, begins to escape convention and to endorse liberal programmes. But even in England and the United States, hundreds of people within the Church are alienated by her timidity and her parrot-like echo of the lower ethics of the State. They turn from her in contempt; they leave the shelter of her altars, and join the noble army of heretics who through the ages, in similar pain and wrath, have tried the ever-futile experiment of separation. For the great loss, to themselves and to us, who is responsible? Largely as usual the Catholic Church, drugged by her own philanthropies, clogged with worldliness since the fatal gift of Constantine, and never even when best-intentioned able to move swiftly enough to meet the righteous impatience of those whose ears have been opened

Social Sin

to the cry of all the oppressions done under the sun.

Yet the nobler Christian mind has expressed itself clearly of late years, on this duty of penitence. Even during the War, this note was struck. The Federal Council of the Churches of Christ in America said:—

"The fact that such a calamity as this world-war could come compels a rigorous scrutiny of the underlying principles of our civilization. It is a summons to the Christian Church to challenge a social order based on mutual distrust and selfish competition. It is a summons in penitence to renounce and oppose the principles of national aggrandizement at the expense of other peoples, of economic selfishness seeking to control the world's resources, trade routes, and markets. It is a summons to the Christian discipleship to bring forth the fruits of repentance in labor for a new world-order."

Fine expressions came from the Christian press of England:—

"Ours is the sin of a Christendom which confesses Christ but will not have Him to reign; which has limited His authority to private occasions and has excluded it in public and social affairs; a Christendom which has told Christ to mind His own business (which is the saving of souls), and to let society and the world alone. Germany perfected that sin: are we free from it?" . . .

"It is a clique of madmen in every country that have driven Europe to this. But what has given them their chance is the diffusion of a compromised Christianity."[1]

Such testimony might be multiplied; but noble words from Gilbert Murray may fitly end this chain of witnesses:—

"The best result that I expect from America's entrance into the war is . . . that in the upbuilding of democracy and permanent peace throughout the world, America and Great Britain will take their part together, united at last by the knowledge that they stand for the same causes, by a common danger and a common ordeal, and, I will venture to add, by a common consciousness of sin."

Looking back over recent years, we can see if we will how habitually we fell into the sin of the Pharisee. The temptation was great; Germany had "got far ahead of the rest in the journey to the abyss " But it was our stern and obvious Christian duty,—the chief duty one would suppose which the Christian Church as such had to

[1] W. Orchard: The Outlook for Religion.

perform in the heated atmosphere of war,—to fasten thought on our own sins rather than on those of our enemy. To make a desperate stand against the country which honestly avowed a Pagan theory seemed necessary to most people, though amazing asperity was shown to the pure-hearted idealists who felt all violence false to the Teachings of the Master. But it was all the more incumbent on those who furthered the war to be sure that our own national life was free 'from what we condemned. When Americans read of the cruelties inflicted by Germans on their prisoners, they had no right to turn their minds away with apologetic distaste from the dastardly murder in the United States of an innocent man who had committed no sin but that of bearing a German name: or complacently to ignore the hanging up by the wrists and flogging of conscientious objectors at Leavenworth. When we shuddered at German atrocities, we should have faced the spectacle of workingmen, many of them with liberty bonds in their pockets, seized like cattle and deported on false pretenses; or the worse spectacle of a minister of Christ who had defended the liberties of the people, taken into a wood, stripped naked, and flogged: or the arrest of Christian Pacifists in Los Angeles while they were singing the twenty-third psalm. When our nerves quivered with the insolent lawlessness that prevailed in Belgium, it had been well to remember the refusal to grant a second trial to Tom Mooney, confessedly condemned on perjured testimony: or if we could bear it, negro lynchings. History moves swiftly nowadays: incidents are readily forgotten, more readily when they concern us, alas, than when they concern our foes! But when we mourn as still we mourn over the ruthless destruction of domestic life across the sea, let us recall the hideous and chronic devastation of family life by industrial slavery, tolerated by most of us with callous indifference or at best with sentimental and ineffective regret.

These thoughts are painful, but they are Christian and necessary; for unless we fought not as self-righteous against guilty but as penitent against impenitent we had no business to fight at all.

"Holy Jesu, grant us tears,
Fill us with heart-searching fears,
Ere that day of doom appears.

Lord, on us Thy Spirit pour,
Kneeling lowly at Thy door,
Ere it close forevermore."

The aftermath of the war, not yet fully reaped, is bitter to us all.

"None ever hated in the world, but came
    To every likeness of the foe he fought,"

These incisive words of Æ. come home with terrible force.

"What wilt thou that I should do unto thee?"

"Lord, that I may receive my sight."

Is the Lenten message one of warning and rebuke alone? Does it leave us permanently plunged in deadening shame? Or has it constructive suggestion?

The answer comes at once in the principle of the Fast: than which, paradoxically, no answer could be at this point more constructive. Personal lives can be purified by resolute abstinence and prayer, till they become instruments of social salvation. The disciplines to which Lent calls are no self-centred indulgence in the quest for private holiness; they are more than preparation for that "Sight of Soul" the mystic craves; they are a preparation for citizenship.

How sadly failure to accept this idea vitiates the effectiveness of many unchurched radicals! The distaste which good Christians often feel for certain radical groups is the radicals' own

fault. They have flung defiance at the traditions
of their fathers, these young socialists and syn-
dicalists; they look to far horizons, they are swing-
ing us today toward a future we know not. But
as they go, they discard contemptuously the
slow achievement of the Christian ages in the art
of personal living. Of restraints, of disciplines,
they will often have none,—unless it be a question
of athletics. Their eyes full of visions, their
hearts full of license, they seek to create a socialist
society on the basis of untrammelled personal
freedom; and they will never succeed. Personal
indulgence is a poor preparation for the difficult
experiment of fraternity.

We are apparently advancing all over the world
from a society based on mastership to one based
on fellowship, and far from relaxing any of our
abstentions and disciplines we shall have to
sharpen them. For fellowship is the hardest of
adventures. It can only be achieved by people
far advanced in self-subordination, in whom the
impulse of unregenerate human nature to have
its own way has been supplanted by the carefully
developed intuition of the Whole. The old interior training of the Christian life was admirably
adapted to further this end. It produced unselfish and self-controlled people; if it is tossed on
the scrap-heap and replaced by easy-going prac-

tises and a defiant claim to follow one's own will, any socialist community will make shipwreck.

The Church, equally occupied with a personal and with a social ideal, strikes the note of the Fast all through the Lenten Sundays. For fasting of course means just training; and training is necessary to any form of energetic life.

Fasting is not argued about in the Bible. Christ does not enjoin it, He assumes it. *"When ye fast,"* He says,—not, Be sure you do fast. And the first thing to be careful about when we fast is not to be of a sad countenance. Cheerfulness is the elementary duty of a person who is practising self-denial. Unworldliness, or detachment as it is sometimes called, is another. "Lay not up for yourselves treasures upon earth," says the Ash-Wednesday Gospel; not because it is wicked to accumulate wealth, an idea of which no hint is given, but because we must refrain from that pursuit if we want our hearts to be in Heaven. "For where your treasure is, there will your heart be also"; the implication being that it is impossible to have great possessions on earth without clinging to them.

Cheerfulness and unworldliness in combination are an excellent beginning to the Lenten training; and no one need pretend that they are easy to practise. But the Church has instant help to give her penitents; for on the first Lenten Sunday she leads them into the desert with their Lord.

The great story of the Temptation has a special meaning for those who desire the humility of penitential self-knowledge, and whose hearts are set on furthering a better social order. They, too, are driven into the wilderness whether they will or no; for we may well remember the words of Carlyle· "Our wilderness is the wide world in an atheistic century." It is when the sense of vocation and purpose inundate our soul that the trial is sure to come. Christ has been here before us. Immediately after the chrism of the Spirit had awakened His Messianic consciousness, awed and possessed by His purpose to establish the Kingdom of God and to save the world, He withdraws to form His plans in solitary communion with the Father. And in the wilderness He meets,—the devil.

Who that has kept a Retreat at some solemn crisis of his life does not understand? These are the times of danger. The devil approached Jesus, as he approaches most of us, not through evil impulses but through channels innocent and good; and as we watch the Perfect Man at odds with fierce temptation, we learn to discriminate, and to discard various insidious popular methods of reaching noble ends. The Master stands firm.

His strength is rooted, not in His own intuitions but in humble acceptance of authority, in the ancient record of the Will of God. There shall be no yielding to mere physical necessity and no claiming of special privilege; no rash and fatuous appeal to sensation; no compromise with evil for the sake of a pure end. The high but unsafe way of the fanatic, the low accredited way of conformity, are alike closed by the last two temptations. Not even the noblest aim to spread God's Kingdom can justify either. These are temptations of the consecrated and disciplined soul; none the less they come from the Evil One.

Even to win the world for Christ, His followers may use no method which He rejected. The lesson is hard; and the Lenten teaching is severe from start to finish. The Epistle for this first Lenten Sunday points out the way for those who are "workers together with Him." It is the way of suffering, patience, and activity, of intelligence and love,—strangely different from the conventional way of amiable and innocuous religiosity. It is salutary to enquire whether one can claim the apostle's words as a description of one's own life: "As dying, and, behold we live; as chastened, and not killed; as sorrowful, yet always rejoicing; as poor, yet making many rich; as having nothing, and yet possessing all things." We are not apostles, yet it is probable that the Church puts the passage where it is with some idea of stimulating us to imitation.

The Gospels for Lent II and III deepen our recognition of the fierce conflict with the mysterious powers of spiritual darkness, carried on by Our Lord through all His ministry. The last Epiphany Sunday has already introduced us to that conflict, in the story of the Gadarene Demoniac; now, through the Lenten period, the Powers of Darkness literally "prowl and prowl around." Both Gospels deal with demoniac possession, which certainly, whatever interpretation be given to it, represents the mysterious irruption of spiritual evil into normal life. Christ is of course always victor, and the faith of the Pagan woman from Canaan has the honor of helping or forcing Him to save. The Gospel for the third Sunday is a strange and awe-inspiring one, suggesting the unseen drama from which are projected like shadows the earthly events which we are privileged to watch. In its plain statement that devils are not cast out through Beelzebub,, but through the finger of God, and that negative repentance and reform are worse than nothing, are implied important principles both for private and for social guidance.

The two Epistles for Lent II and III, like the

Epistle for Lent I, turn from the combat of the Captain of our salvation, to the combat of His followers; and very directly and practically single out two sins for special warning. The two are Impurity and Covetousness, Lust and Greed. Here are indeed the root sins of civilization: deep bedded in individual hearts, but bearing evil fruit for society when they are matured. To set the community free from the sins of the flesh and the sins of the acquisitive will,—there indeed is the programme for every movement of social reform; and in pursuing the programme it is well to remember the warning of the Gospel: not to force on society a negative virtue, lest its last state be worse than its first; but to supplement all cleansing and exorcism, by strong constructive work. Whether in regard to the social evil, to intemperance, or to that other sin of eager profit-making ("which is idolatry," says Paul succinctly), the same principle holds: In proportion as the evils are discredited or forbidden, a Christian civilization must hasten to fill their place with positive interests, inspiration and joy.

In these Lenten Sundays, we are thus inevitablv led outward again, from the thought of personal discipline to the social aspects of evil; for the sins which Lent fights poison society as they poison the soul.

Self-disciplines are not the end of obedience; they are the beginning. The religious man must became enlightened, penitent, purified; but in proportion as he attains, he must enter the sad sanctuary of corporate penitence, and corporate penitence, on penalty of producing despair, must end in corporate action.

The Church has too largely forgotten the force of her own formulæ and the lesson she inherited from the prophets. She has concerned herself all but exclusively with the personal aspects of virtue, and has continually repeated the half-truth, that converted individuals will automatically create a converted society; meanwhile, the radicals shout back at her that other half-truth, that a decent society makes decent men. The individualism which modern Christianity is just beginning to outgrow, is responsible for the contemptuous distaste with which the revolution is prone to treat the power that should as many think be its best ally. And this individualism has given excuse to critics like Lowes Dickinson and John Stuart Mill to see in Christianity a separatist, egotistic and negative ideal, which if widely followed would involve the suicide of civilization.

As between the radicals and the Church, a Christian must think that the Church holds the more fundamental truth. But each half-truth needs the other. "Lead us not into temptation," says the Lord's own prayer. The words involve a definite political and social policy, a statesman-ship lofty enough to create a society where the low incentives to lay up treasure on earth shall be supplanted by incentives of honor and serv-ice, and where the all but irresistible pressure to disobey Christ by taking thought for the morrow shall be removed. The pitfalls awaiting feeble pilgrims, due to the system in which we are en-tangled, must be swept out of the way by a con-verted race.

For only a converted race, possessed by pas-sionate social penitence, invigorated and emanci-pated through the disciplines of self-control, can abandon itself with any hope of success to this great end. Humanity must rise to new heights of disciplined sacrifice. . . . And as it listens hesi-tant to the call from far horizons of vision, the devil renews his lures. He whispers that per-sonal holiness is the only legitimate aim for a Christian, everything else being irrelevant; that you can't make people good by legislation; that there must be a different law for states and men; and that industrial and political security are best obtained by willingness to make a little compromise and to fall down and worship him.

We are not to blame if our secret hearts are puzzled, and tempted to respond. The literal expression of the love which is the outcome of penitence is not always easy in personal behavior; but it seems hopelessly difficult in group-life. One may be personally a non-resistant; but when other people are attacked shall one not defend them?

Trustees have duties, even if it should happen that protecting the property of their wards involves opposition to the demands of underpaid workmen. . . . That complicated impulse, the desire for national expansion, includes an honest desire for the welfare of millions of people.—And so on, *ad infinitum.*

Before this vision of a penitent race, bending all its energy of mind and will to make the laws of brotherhood the base of civilization, thought grows dizzy and faith all but fails. The problem is so intricate, the need for regeneration so deep. And there is such a fearful lack of precedent Men have tried, now and then. The Pilgrim Fathers tried; but their theocracy was hardly fulfilled in brotherly love. In a sense, the Bolsheviki are trying; and their amazing experiment may give Christianity a chance it has never had before; but it is all too evident that they have never

been with Christ in the wilderness. Many hopes
are turning to British Labor, which published the
famous programme that released the laws of
Christ perhaps for the first time into practical
politics. But British Labor, like American, is at
this writing divided against itself. To formulate
ideals is easy; to acclaim them is not difficult. But
to follow them and give them practical application
is another matter. Where shall we look for our
dynamic?

Not to the political world. Antagonists without and within,—decorous antagonists, many of
them, smooth-spoken and benevolent,—unite to
sneer down any attempt at an idealistic reading
of history. Where are examples to be found even
of effort to get the law of love into the social and
political structure? Instances can be found in
Christendom of disinterested treatment of backward or feeble people; though the cynic insists
that instances of plain predatory behavior,
lightly camouflaged, are more frequent. But of
distinctly Christian behavior toward the equal
and strong, or toward the conquered foe, on the
part of Christian nations, examples are few indeed. Certainly the post-war European world
does not furnish them. "In honour preferring
one another," ran the Apostolic injunction. What

an extraordinary thing it would be to see a nation follow the .precept! Helpless, discouraged, desperate in presence of the world-spectacle, we are almost ready to abandon our dream.

Helpless? . When "God is reigning from the Tree"?

Our sins crush us to the ground. By the time the fourth Lenten Sunday is reached, refreshment is sadly needed; and the Church at this point pauses with her own tender wisdom to give us the assurance of strength and hope. Though we be tied and bound by the chain of our sins, the Epistle tells us of a Free City, the mother of us all,—Jerusalem which is Above, whereof we are the children and the citizens. Though we have starved our brothers, the Gospel tells us of Him Who fed the Five Thousand and Who shall feed them, and us; it promises food for body as for soul, and carries to every devout heart the all-comforting suggestion of the Eucharistic Feast.

Then, having assured satisfaction for those two primal needs, Freedom and Nourishment, the Church turns her children on Passion Sunday to face the Holy Cross. "Vexilla Regis Prodeunt," she sings:

"O Tree of Glory, Tree most fair,
Ordained those holy limbs to bear!

As by the Cross Thou dost restore,
So rule and guide us evermore."

There on the "Glory-Tree," as the old Anglo-Saxon poets loved to call it, Love Crucified forever saves the world. We turn away from our poor puzzled efforts, from our weak contrition, to the power of Him Who sinless bare our sins in His own Body: away from sin to salvation, away from self to Christ. Until this point, the Christian Year has held us to contemplation of His words and deeds; now as we enter Passion-Tide she bids us contemplate His very Person, in His atoning pain.

The Epistle for the fifth Sunday in Lent, commonly called Passion-Sunday, is a solemn passage from Hebrews. It draws to a climax all those deep intuitions of sacrifice which have wrought in the heart of the race from prehistoric times, and which humanity, however modern and enlightened, tries in vain to escape. In Him Who is "Himself the Victim and Himself the Priest," these prophetic intuitions find their final satisfaction. "Christ being come an high-priest of good things to come" (even of the

Kingdom of Justice which shall be), "entered in once into the Holy Place, having obtained eternal redemption for us." We must be saved before we can be saviours, we who are so eager to reform the world. And salvation instantly responds to penitence. In the Gospel from St. John, the Master Himself reassures His own, by averring His eternal Being and power.

As on Passion Sunday we enter the inner sanctuary of the Christian Year and of our holy faith, the veiled Cross on the altar says to us: "This darkness is the light of the World."

CHAPTER VI: PASSION-TIDE

Antiphon: In all their affliction He was afflicted, and the angel of His presence saved them.

V. Let this mind be in you

R. Which was also in Christ Jesus.

Almighty God, we beseech Thee graciously to behold this Thy family, for which our Lord Jesus Christ was contented to be betrayed and given up into the hands of wicked men, and to suffer death upon the Cross; Who now liveth and reigneth with Thee and the Holy Ghost ever, one God, world without end.   Amen.

CHAPTER VI: PASSION-TIDE

TO the initiate, Christianity shines supreme among world-religions as the Faith of the Cross; but it is with humble dread that any mind seeks to speak to others of the central mystery of Love. What is there in that plain symbol, two pieces of wood at right angles, which however casually seen quickens adoration? The springs of tears are loosened by the shrines encountered in ancient lands,—at the wayside, in Alpine pastures, on some horror-stricken battle-field. But a telegraph pole at twilight will often do as well, or the accidental snow-scars on a mountain slope or the upward pointing twigs of a little balsam tree: as indeed, by the Tree of the Cross all trees are consecrate. The Christian heart loves to find crosses everywhere: to see in the centre of the Passion-Flower, in the stars of the northern sky, the Sign of our redemption.

Yet in spite of such rare hints in the visible world, nature does not love crosses. Their sharp limitations are alien to her instinct for soft-flowing endless lines, and forms shaped by the free necessities of their being. Whatever dim suggestions of sacrifice and surrender the natural order may contain, the Law of the Cross essentially transcends nature. And in the insensible slipping back to the levels of natural religion which has marked the last century and a half, the Cross has been largely discredited. Whole religious systems deliberately discard it, and an intense revulsion from all the dogmatic formulæ which once gathered around the Atonement has been experienced even by the orthodox.

But the reaction has spent itself. The law of Sacrifice, working vitally at the centre of conscious personal and social life, is recapturing the allegiance of religious minds.

And rightly; for here is the consummation of the religion of the Incarnation,—here, where the Infinite is revealed at the last stage of its self-emptying which is its true fulfillment, claiming every prerogative of finiteness. In vain modern instinct finds the Cross ghastly, painful, intolerable; in vain modern theory accounts for faith in sacrifice by tracing the dim gropings of the fear-stricken primitive mind. No evasion is possible; the Suffering God in evident reality hangs forever on the Rood of Time,—our eyes behold Him there. If God enters the temporal order at all,—which He must, since He is Love,—He can not stop short in being born, or in manifesting the divine Nature through deeds of might and mercy;[1] He can stop nowhere till He perfect His infinitude by bowing to defeat and death, till He sound the depths of absolute self-identification with His universe, till He bear our sins in His own Body on the Tree, and appeal, not only to our adoration but our compassion.

So Calvary completes Bethlehem. It shows forth to all ages God entering the order of history in the only way possible to Him in a sin-sick world.

And the story of the Entrance is in this stage as elsewhere entirely simple and realistic. If one can read with fresh eyes the narrative of the Passion as the Church with solemn iteration spreads it before us from every Gospel source, in full detail, during Holy Week, it becomes appallingly evident how love finds itself done to death by the normal social forces which are at once the result and the support of individual sins.

Jesus never courted death. That His Agony has redemptive value is deep and mystic truth, but He did not live to die, as Roman teaching has sometimes assumed; He lived to establish the Kingdom of God. "To this end have I been

[1] See note, p. 51.

born,''—not that I might save men by dying
but "that I should bear witness unto the truth.''
Humanly speaking, He wanted to carry out His
purpose, and sweat those great drops of blood
because He saw that He was not to be permitted
to do so in the way that He had hoped. Since
the world is what it is, His witness led to the
Cross. He knew this too, knew it at least from
the moment of His transfiguration, when in the
excellent glory the great exponents of law and
prophecy, of righteous order and holy aspiration,
of tradition and hope, spake with Him of His de-
cease which He should accomplish at Jerusalem.

The forces which crucify love are rarely those
of open evil. In the time of Jesus, they were
the due ecclesiastical authorities, and also the in-
tellectuals, and the representatives of law and
government, of all the institutions which are the
honorable basis of a stable and respectable civilization. And they were no worse than usual.
Nevertheless, they combined with one accord to
try by proper legal machinery and with accredited
decorum to execute the Lord of Glory. He was
executed as a common criminal; and the mob,
probably disappointed and angered because He
had refused to lead a popular political revolution,
was on the side of the executioners.

All this is not pleasant to contemplate, and

it is quite different from what we choose and like to expect. Men are always looking for patent wickedness, which can be opposed by crystal-clear and self-righteous satisfaction. With what sacrificial heroism they would fight it! How gladly would they suffer the last penalty, and die storming its dark citadel! But that is not how things happen. Indeed, if a cause appears luminously and picturesquely right, it needs to be very carefully examined, for it is under suspicion. The really best causes, the worth-while causes, the causes of the future, are always on trial at the bar of the world, and always by the world scorned and condemned.

No devils appeared to condemn and crucify the Lord of Love. Cunning devils! They worked through human instruments, who deceived themselves systematically, and all meant extremely well. Even Judas was a disciple, probably no worse than an impatient one, who wanted to force the hand of his perplexing leader. As for the Pharisees and Sadducees, Pilate, Herod,—all the long pageant of figures on whom falls the central shadow of history,—they were fairly conscientious people, with mixed motives like the rest of us; they all told themselves that they acted for the best good of the community. And there is doubtless a reason why the Lord should have been crucified between two robbers. The reformer who seeks to make all things new is always confused by the public with the agitator and thief who would ravage society. In watching those who are notorious in one's own day, it behooves one to be careful.

It can not be too often repeated: the academic, the religious, the official, and the popular world, united to condemn the Saviour. It condemns its saviours still.

Or has the situation changed? One pauses and wonders. Certainly it is not what Christ expected. We are very comfortable today, we Christians, and inveterately respectable. Is our condition at all dangerous? Is there a bare possibility that we have slipped over to the side of Pilate and the Pharisees?

No one demands that men should court disgrace or defeat, or exalt pain to a morbid eminence as they have sometimes appeared to do. Jesus never did any of these things. But He did adopt an attitude which brought Him straight to Golgotha, and it never entered His mind, so far as the evidence shows, that the Society He founded or the individuals who followed Him could escape a similar fate. The sharp distinction which set His disciples apart from the world, as salt, as leaven, as a city set on a hill, pervades the Gospels. The

last Beatitude, which promises the same blessing
as to the poor in spirit, is for the persecuted, and
the phrase does not run that men are blessed *if*
they are persecuted for righteousness sake, but
when,—a fact which has caused great perplexity
to sundry small students of the Bible, who were
obliged in honesty to confess that they were never
persecuted at all. The last High-Priestly prayer
expressly says that in the world we shall have tribulation, and that we are not of the world just as
Christ is not of the world. We are to drink of
His cup and be baptized with His baptism.
Wherein have we failed? How shall we be baptized with that baptism today?

Christ dies, be it noted, not as Victim, but as
Saviour. The Cross shows forth, not primarily
endurance or patient acquiescence in sacrifice, but
defiance of the existing social and religious order.
Passive resistance if you will: "Put up again thy
sword into its place": but resistance not acquiescence; and resistance to the uttermost, lifted high
on that Hill of death which is the sky-line of the
planet.

The entire story of Holy Week breathes this
quality in Christ of defiance and resistance.
Whether He head on Palm Sunday a political
demonstration which might easily have turned into
popular revolt, or overthrow peaceful commerce

in the Temple courts, or publicly denounce in scathing terms the sins of lawyers and religious leaders, the positive, daring, dangerous nature of His actions is so clear that one can not wonder if men took Him for a demagogue. His opposition ended in defeat and open shame. But it is the world's salvation.

"Let this mind be in you, which was also in Christ Jesus," says the Palm-Sunday Epistle: placed by the Church at the entrance to the great Week, to warn us that we are not only to love and adore the Captain of our salvation as we watch Him made perfect through suffering, but also to be conformed to His likeness, to follow in His Way. Let this mind be in us which was in Christ Jesus. Dare we say Amen to that?

There is another aspect of Christ's Passion, perhaps more familiar, also deep in social import, of which one would not for a moment minimize the sacred reality. This is the aspect dear to the secret heart of all Christian people, who when suffering or oppressed venture to take to themselves the amazing phrase of Scripture, and to believe that through their voluntary offering of pain, they may "fill up that which is lacking of the afflictions of Christ," and so bear their heroic part in the work of redemption. Surely their faith is justified. It is the glory of Christianity to teach that love is made strong in weakness, and that the defeated and the feeble rather than the valiant and victorious are most intimately one with their Lord. The Napoleons are not the world's real saviours; no, but rather the obscure and patient souls battered into insignificance, tortured by the little woes which are the worst, inhibited, paralyzed, beaten, forgotten.

By the divine paradox of the Cross we know that these experiences may not be ignominious waste, but may connote the richest productive and creative values. People subject to them need suffer no lack of inward dignity, need hold no shrinking attitude of apology or shame: it is theirs in the hidden sanctuary whence flow the forces of salvation, to be united with the Lord of Love and Life. Nay, even the sinner, if he is penitent, may lift his broken but cleansed existence upon that Cross "where He in flesh our flesh who made, our sentence bore, our ransom paid."

Men have long tried to throw discredit on the idea of vicarious atonement, but they can not discredit vicarious suffering, for that is not a theory but a fact. It is part of the social bond which unites the human race. In every factory where children work, in every devastated village of France or Armenia, in every home where unnoted sacrifice or pain shines gently till its light is spent, the innocent suffer for the guilty. Christianity does not invent this suffering; it brings consolation by investing with a possible spiritual glory what was often taken by Pagan life as a badge of shame. Vicarious suffering is sure to prevail more and more as sympathy widens and vibrations pass more readily, as they begin to do, from group to group. The fortunate are not excluded from this privilege, since the Son of God was not. "Agonies are one of my changes of garments," says Walt Whitman· "I do not ask the wounded person how he feels, I myself become the wounded person."[1] To "become the wounded person" is the chief hidden comfort of many who live perforce at ease, with the joys of Nature, love, work and art healthfully open to them, while yet their hearts are bowed under the burden of the cost of these good things to their brothers who labor. In the secret steady pain, ever present though of course often subconscious, in which the life of the just man when he is tenderhearted must today be passed, lies the earnest of a better future.

To Christian thought, the suffering of the innocent, whether voluntary or enforced, is not futile. The last ignominy of uselessness does not rest on it; perhaps always, surely whenever the voluntary

[1] Whitman: Song of Myself.

element enters, it is the seed of expiation from which the Tree of Healing shall spring. By uplifting vicarious suffering into potential vicarious atonement, the Faith of the Cross releases men from one of the most cruel burdens which oppress their mortal destiny. O marvel of heavenly grace, which transforms the anguish of the world into its redemption!

But to recognize this transformation is not to become reconciled to cruelty and wrong. If we yield to that temptation, we entangle ourselves in one of the cleverest and subtlest webs ever woven by the Adversary for the beguiling of the faithful. Christianity a fatalistic acquiescence in circumstance, a morbid exaltation of pain! How the accusation rings through modern times, from John Stuart Mill to Nietzsche! And how often the "otherworldly" attitude of Christians, with their flight from active warfare, has corroborated it! Yet mere submission, or even escape from the struggle with the world, the flesh and the devil on spiritual wings, never was Christ's way. Had it been, there had been no Trial, no Cross, no revelation of His Risen Might. In the still tug-of-war between good and evil, good always turns evil to its own purposes, which is the reason why this game of cosmic forces can excite the angels' laughter, and is consonant with their celestial bliss: but evil is evil just the same, and to be overcome, if may be, in the open.

War, for instance, may purify the race, or at least be the occasion for glorious devotions, but war is none the less a horrible thing, which decent men today are seeking to end forever. So guiltless suffering, especially when it springs from the fellowship of love, may have redemptive power; but the causes of it are not to be encouraged for that reason. The Cross meets the problem of pain by a double method. It exalts the devout and perhaps even the innocent sufferer to a mystic union with the Saving Victim Who opens wide the gate of heaven: and at the same time it hurls defiance in the only possible effective way, which is the way of all-subduing love, at the sin which has caused that pain.

While autocracies ruled the world, the first method was the more usual; sacrificial faith centred naturally in the ideal of endurance. As democracy matures, the second method must assert itself; sacrificial faith must centre in aggressive action. We must become Crusaders, appropriating to nobler ends all the old metaphors of warfare. And it is to the Body Corporate, no less than to private persons, that the call is sounding.

Individuals have always known the Divine Se-

cret in its double aspect; they have not wholly
failed to hear the summons of the Cross to noble
deed. Defiance of wrong has not been lacking
through the Christian ages; it gives the Church
her martyrs, the world some at least of her heroes.
But it has never fulfilled the social will of the
Master, Who habitually viewed His followers as
a group, a fellowship, acting with perfect solidarity in a distinctive way. The apostle could see
the Cross as the great social solvent, breaking
down partitions, of race and sex and class, of bond
and free, of Jew and Gentile, and restoring all
men to unity in Him Who is our Peace. Perhaps an individualistic interpretation devoid of
any vision of corporate sacrifice, is the reason
why Christendom has so inadequately realized the
grand ideal; why in this year of grace 1921, the
principle of rational internationalism has to fight
for its life, and the class-struggle threatens bit-
terer and more penetrating war than any the race
has known.

What can avert the threat except the Cross of
Christ? Men have tried all else, this they have
never tried; nor will they do so except by supernatural grace.

"For an earlier generation, the Cross was a
redemptive act by which God and man were reconciled: and so it is, but the Cross of Calvary was

such an act only because it contained within itself the infinite potentialities which history is slowly revealing. Then for a later generation it came to be conceived as the moral power for reforming personal character. For us it must be the over-throwing of barriers and the reconstruction of a new order of social and national life." [1]

The new life for which men long will not come without cost. Sacrifice alone can bring it to the birth. Individual sacrifice, forever necessary, is insufficient in these days of group action, involved in the free movements of democracy. Corporate sacrifice is essential to the redemption of the body politic. In what direction can it be looked for?

Three possibilities suggest themselves: the sacrifice of a class, of a nation, of a Church. Consider each in turn.

Class-sacrifice: why not? In the modern pressure toward socializing and equalizing wealth, imagine the propertied and privileged classes taking the lead, under the impulse of a new chivalry; supporting, nay initiating legislation which would destroy their every privilege. Picture the people who make war-profits proposing schemes of taxation to absorb those profits entirely; owners of

[1] W. Orchard: The Outlook for Religion, p. 193. Funk & Wagnalls, 1918.

large fortunes inventing laws for restraint of the methods by which such fortunes can be made, and endorsing the tendencies deeper than laws which will render disparities of wealth impossible. Picture great corporations declining to use non-union labor, hastening to give labor a share not only in profits but in control, and facing gladly all the dislocation, temporary loss, and incertitude implied in the new experiments in industrial democracy. In a word, picture all well-to-do folk, full of social compunction and prophetic zeal, insisting that it be given unto the last as unto the first, albeit they represent the "first," and joyously establishing the universal poverty which alone can inherit the kingdom of Heaven, and which in a very literal sense must probably accompany the creation of the commonwealth of Christian dreams.

Now all this is not nearly so impossible to imagine as it would have been ten years ago. Faint instances of such spirit and attitude can be found, quite widely spread: in the proposals of a group of Quaker employers, in the magnanimous policies of many individual manufacturers, in the rapid diffusion of the new ideas of shop committees and industrial control. It is true that Fear, a stern but sometimes salutary schoolmaster, has something to do with this apparent change, as

men of concentrated power watch the advance
of the Red Flag; but it is surely legitimate to think
that the long education in social compunction and
democratic ideals which has been in process for
the last century and a half, has something more.
Nor may we brand all hesitation and industrial
conservatism as due to selfish greed. Far from it:
the trustee's sense of responsibility is a disinterested impulse, and the fear lest in seeking to
remedy rotten construction we pull down the whole
building and leave an unsheltered humanity to
cower in the ruins, is ever present to most minds
in control of social affairs.

Yet with all allowances, and all mitigations and
exceptions made, the leading features of the spectacle when seen from a certain distance, are unmis-
takable. The classes in possession appear obstinately clinging to their every prerogative: capital-
istic interests manipulating politics behind the
scenes, manufacturers repeating their old parrot
cry, "nothing to arbitrate," wealth and privilege
everywhere righteously shocked at any hint of disturbance of the *status quo*. "Aliens" from every
class will doubtless combine in any onward movement; that a class as a whole should pass a self-
denying ordinance and legislate its privileges out
of existence, or even, with an impulse of disinterested devotion, limit its own power appreciably,

is an idea to be entertained, one fears, only by philosophers who live in the country Through the Looking Glass. One does not need to be an economic determinist to despair of any class-sacrifice on a large scale.

The unchristian doctrine of the class-struggle unluckily has history on its side. Proletarian dictatorship, abhorrent to most Anglo-Saxons, finds justification in its own eyes, from the honest conviction that no substantial justice is to be looked for from classes in possession. And those who hate the theory worst are helpless to point out instances on a large scale where any class has ever acted of its own free will against its own interests.

Well then, how about the sacrifice of a nation? A crucified state: waiving its own claims in favor of the prosperity of its late enemy or even of its allies.

"I confess that I dream of the day when an English statesman shall arise with a heart too large for England, having courage in the face of his countrymen to assert of some suggested policy: 'This is good for your trade, it is necessary for your domination, but it will vex a people farther off; it will profit nothing to the general humanity; therefore away with it!' . . . When a British minister dares to speak so, and when a British public applauds him speaking, then shall the nation be so glorious that her praise, instead of exploding from within from loud civil mouths, shall come to her from without, as all worthy praise must, from the alliances she has fostered and from the populations she has saved."[1] So, in mid nineteenth century, wrote the woman-seer Mrs. Browning.

"If it is not beneath the Cross of Jesus that nations will lay down their arms, it may be by revolution among the armies and rebellion among the workers. If we can not secure the ending of War by the blood of the Cross, other blood may flow which will not cleanse, but only cry out for blood the more."[2]

It is entirely possible to conceive a nation discarding the wisdom of this world in favor of treatment of a hostile power with the most energetic policies which love could invent: so full of magnanimous and unselfish solicitude for the general welfare that it could interpret the Mind of Christ to the whole world. Suppose the policies of love to fail, as they probably would for a time,—picture the nation exalting itself by the common will to a Cross of shame; accepting national defeat even to the point of subjection, and loss of all its

[1] Mrs. Browning: Poems Before Congress. Preface.
[2] Orchard: The Outlook for Religion, p. 250.

economic ambition and political pride. . . No, one has certainly not seen that picture in the after-war negotiations: to be entirely frank, few people would want to.

Why not, would take long to discuss. But turn away from these two conceptions, one unlikely, the other distasteful, and try again. Consider the picture of a crucified Church.

"It may need a crucified Church to bring a crucified Christ before the eyes of the world": [1] that is the end of the quotation from England given on a preceding page. And an echo comes from America:

"What can the Church do to be saved? is a question which many Churchmen are asking themselves, and the answer comes strangely close to the New Testament parallel. The apostolic order, the deposit of faith, the rule of life, and all the traditions of the past,—all these she has carefully kept from her youth up, but there still seems to be something lacking to the fulfilment of her true place in the heart of the world. It may be that she still needs to sell what she has and give to the poor, and accept her Master's Cross." "We talk of the Church as the extension of the Incarnation, but just as the latter was not com-

[1] Orchard: The Outlook for Religion.

plete until Calvary, so the Church will not have completed her identification until she has given herself completely for the life of the world." [1]

It is sadly easy to regard the whole Christian achievement in the light of irony: faint and far sounds the call of the Cross in Christian ears. Our salt has lost its savor, our light is very dim, our city is set on no hill, but in philistine comfort among the cities of the plain. The Church has become all but indistinguishable from the world. With terror we remember how, in the first century, Church conspired with nation to put Jesus to death. Let us passionately resolve that history shall not repeat itself. The mind may well dwell for a moment on the haughty Church of the middle ages, still, in these later days, clinging desperately to the phantom of her temporal power: on her wealthy prelates, her vast endowments, her bitter fight for supremacy with temporal rulers. Since the Reformation, the picture is in some respects less dark; yet still the good works of the Church cling like a millstone around her neck as she struggles for freedom. It is for their sakes that many of her excellent officials, succumbing to the Temptation in the Wilderness, compromise with the Powers that Be.

And then, let us picture the Church, the mystical

[1] Right Reverend Paul Jones.

Body of Christ, His own Body wherein He still bears the sins of the world. The Church as she might be: no longer watchful over her own prerogatives or possessions, even for the sake of her missions or her charities; watchful rather to gather her children from every nation into one great unity of love, that they may live by a law which the world denies: bound to follow that law literally in political, social, religious, industrial relations,—and to take the consequences when active obedience is rendered impossible. Let her fling one mighty challenge to the principles which have wrecked the nations. Let her find the forces of this world opposing and persecuting her; not as now, endorsing her or seeking her favor. Let her be decried, repressed, ridiculed, by intellectual leaders, commercial magnates, religious authorities. Let her stubbornly decline the compromises they offer,—cry aloud in the wilderness to suspicious and secretive nations the law of candor, to hostile peoples the law of forgiveness, to rival interests the law of love. And then let her welcome the results sure to follow, and take the eleventh chapter of Hebrews as the Magna Carta of her liberties.

Could the Church boldly adopt this line of action, she would indeed be filled with citizens of that Jerusalem which is above, the mother of the free,—citizens refusing, however tested and wracked, to be disloyal to their native land. In this manner, Christianity might regain reality and save the world. But if she remains in future as in past cautious, hesitant, conventional,—if she bows under the weight of Custom, "heavy as frost and deep almost as life,"—then indeed she is in fearful peril, as her Master warned. Worse than this,—for to do her justice, she can rise above thoughts of her own salvation,—unless she follow Him along His way of pain, the Cross whereon Love reaches out its arms may cease to be the centre of the world's landscape.

Yet, no! For it is God as well as Man who hangs thereon. Corporate sacrifice, of nation, class or Church might save the world; but if we fail Him, He will not fail us. Christ is God and Man: the Church is Christ and clay. In the eternal depths of boundless love, the eternal mystery of redemption proceeds forever, and the Lamb is slain from the foundation of the world. We have not entered the Holy of Holies in dwelling on our union with the Passion and the sacrifice of Christ; in a way we have been claiming too much for ourselves; not more than He bids us claim, indeed, but more than we shall attain. Once more we remind ourselves, that in Passion-Tide we turn from self to the Saviour. He has trodden the winepress alone and of the people there was none with Him. He looked and there was none to help; and He wondered that there was none to uphold. Wherefore His own arm brought salvation. He was once offered to bear the sins of many. Then said He, Lo, I come, to do Thy Will, O God. By the which will we are sanctified, by the offering of the Body of Jesus Christ once for all.

The law of holy social life is the law of sacrifice; but we men who would redeem, all need redemption. Only sinlessness has power perfectly to save, and till the Church is free from sin, she will be Crucifier as well as Crucified. These are the deep thoughts to which we are summoned by the Epistles of Holy Week. Sacrifice, revealed in the finite order, drawing to its law all that would restore the race to its heritage, can be fulfilled only in the Heart of God. It is a social principle only because it is a divine fact. Only strength from the Crucified God can enable men, whether in personal, international or industrial relations, to die to those natural impulses of self-protection and self-expansion which are so plausible and fierce, and having passed through the grave and gate of death to rise to a joyous resurrection.

But if we fail to be wholly "in-oued" with Him upon the Cross, ours may at least be the part of those who watch at the foot, not in derision but in love and grief. Though the Church thrice deny with Peter, yet she may repent with Peter, who was her first Primate. Though she sleep like the disciples at Gethsemane, she may yet stand gazing with the Holy Women at the Sacred Tree. In her wealth and prosperity, even, Christ will not exile her from His Passion; albeit the one sad privilege of that rich man, Joseph of Arimathea, "who also was His disciple," was to prepare His Body for the grave. . Only from the Judas-rôle, Good Lord, deliver her!

The Seven Words, in like manner, are spoken to us before they can be spoken by us. It is we who know not what we do, and who may therefore be forgiven. To our penitence comes the promise of fellowship in Paradise: we receive the exquisite command to form one family. In our awestruck presence, dying Love cries forth His thirst for souls, His darkness of desolation, His consciousness of achievement, and commends Himself to Love Undying. And if at all these points we find also example and model for our own attitude toward enemies and penitents and friends, toward pain, despair and work, we know in our bitter imperfection and our failure to share His redeeming anguish, that what we can not do, God in Christ *↓* achieves, so that we too may enter into the Mys- *Euch.* tery, not as saved alone but also as saviours in our measure. For by one offering, He hath perfected forever them that are sanctified.

Thus social Christianity is rooted in the Catholic faith: thus, obedient, we turn from man to God, from our sins to our Redeemer.

Turn in the confidence of certain hope. The Sacrament of Unity, wherein we are one Bread, but in expectation. ~~Once more, and most im- Church for all ages, not in submission or despair, but in expectation.~~ Once more, and most impressively, is sounded in the Gospel for Wednesday of Holy Week, and in the Epistle for Holy Thursday, the note of the Kingdom to be. At the very moment when the Church bids us commemorate the perpetuity of sacrifice, in the institution of the Blessed Sacrament, she reminds us that such sacrifice is "Till He come " Death is the earnest of life, sacrifice of victory. Nourished by that Heavenly Food, let us leap to the Cross in the heroic spirit of old Anglo-Saxon poetry, assured that here is no sign of accepted defeat, but the pledge of that coming Kingdom of the Father, where Christ shall once more eat of the fruit of the Vine with His beloved, in the Festival of Fellowship.

CHAPTER VII: EASTER-TIDE

Antiphon: He was seen of them forty days, speaking of the things pertaining to the kingdom of God.

V. If ye then be risen with Christ

R. Set your affection on things above.

O God, Who for our redemption didst give Thine only begotten Son to the death of the Cross, and by His glorious resurrection hast delivered us from the power of our enemy; Grant us so to die daily from sin, that we may evermore live with Him in the glory of His resurrection; through the same Christ our Lord.　　Amen.

EASTER morning dawns, and testifies forever that life on the lower level of Nature can never satisfy human need. The "sky behind the sky" must send its messengers; through earthly atmosphere must break the heavenly light.

The necessity for the recurrent witness of life from above, the worthlessness of the social gospel without the spiritual,—this is the first lesson of Easter to the Christian. Yet in the awestruck penetration to new planes of being, fellowship is not for a moment forgotten. As the faithful wait in the hush of Holy Saturday, love reaches out to that "dim place" where the Lord of Life brings release to the expectant multitudes in prison. On no scene has religious art dwelt more tenderly than on the Harrowing of Hell; it shows us patriarchs, prophets, and the unknown dead, pressing rapturously upward on the summons of Him Who descends among them bearing the triumphant banner of the Passion that can redeem even in the shades beyond the tomb.

Meanwhile, the Church on earth in her more ancient rites blessed the elements of the natural order,—salt, oil, water receiving Sacramental power at her hands. She listened to the story of the first creation, now recreated in the Spirit; and still she brings her children to the font, that they may be buried with her Lord in that baptism which is death to sin and new birth to holiness. So the myriads of the Church Expectant, who since the beginning of history have gathered in the land which is very far off, meet in her embrace the generations as they rise.

In the morning comes the spiritual triumph of life immortal,—serene, secret, sweet beyond our dreams. The group-sense is present, but it is for once secondary. Intimate, personal, is the revelation. This garden at dawn, the woman turning to meet the gardener and finding the Lord of the Garden of Souls, the beloved Voice, speaking her own name, the swift response,—these holy joys were not only for Mary, they may be claimed by every child of man. In their divine and homely simplicity they witness to the exquisite nearness of earthly life and the life that is unseen.

But Mother Church will not allow us to lose ourselves in ecstasy of joy and praise. In the heart of the mystical glory echo once more her practical commands. How many have found the end of the glorious Easter Collect disappointing and tame? "Almighty God, Who through Thine Only-Begotten Son Jesus Christ hast overcome death and opened unto us the gates of everlasting life: we humbly beseech Thee that as by Thy special grace preventing us, Thou dost put into our hearts good desires; so by Thy continual help we may bring the same to good effect" . . . The lyric flight which bears us upward on its anapestic beat through open gates to the eternal realm, ends with reiteration of the sober needs of every day.

Mother Church is very wise.

Through the Scriptures for Easter week and the succeeding Sundays runs first and foremost, constant testimony to the amazing fact of the Resurrection, and its power to transform the disciples. But mingled with this, almost anxiously it would seem, are humdrum and outspoken moral injunctions. The Christian mind has never been lost in any dazed and vaporous curiosity about life on other planes. As shown in these Epistles, it dwells on the prosaic levels of ordinary moral struggle,—a region far from beautiful when viewed in the solemn radiance of the eternal Easter. Yet that purifying radiance is streaming like sunlight into the hearts of the faithful, who unfold like flowers in the Garden of God.

For the Risen Life is to be manifest in that supreme adventure,—making people good. The creation of holiness from the poor frail stuff of human nature is the chief concern of those who worship the Risen Lord. Character may never for one moment be neglected for the sake of vision; and character, as Goethe knew, can not be developed in solitude. Nobody, least of all himself, knows anything about the character of the contemplative and solitary. Character is a social product, evoked and tested by human contacts, and the Easter Epistles keep us in the "Strom der Welt."

Sin, in the first Epistle for Easter Sunday, is described with almost shocking plainness. In the terrible list, the two old enemies fought through Lent are stressed once more. Fornication and covetousness, self-indulgence and acquisitiveness, —they are the double curse which rests on society to this day. In the other Easter Day Epistle, Paul in homely metaphor bids us purge out the old leaven. The Epistles for Easter Monday and Tuesday are from sermons on the Resurrection, the first by Peter, the second by Paul. "Of a truth I perceive that God is no respecter of persons," says Peter,—striking that obvious though radical note with evident amaze. It took a vision, in addition to all he had gone through and all he had learned from the Master, to teach that devout Jew to call nothing common or unclean.

John, in the Epistle for the first Sunday after Easter, stresses the life-giving power of faith; but in the Epistles for the second and third Sundays, Peter returns to the ethical note: Peter was not much of a mystic. Yet he rises above platitudes into pure Christian air when he insists that if we are unjustly treated for doing right, we shall be not only patient, but glad and grateful. Any Christian who has experienced even a little the exultation of following in the steps of Him Who "also suffered for us," knows what he means. But Peter's most provocative admonition is when he tells those set free in Christ to submit themselves to every ordinance of man for the Lord's sake. People who have a lurking admiration for the rebel, and are inclined at times to defy rather than submit for the Lord's sake, find this a sweeping injunction, and are tempted to remind us that Peter was never an intellectual light in the Apostolic family. Nevertheless, Peter was right in his basic principle. The Christian democrat has to realize that true liberty can only be fulfilled by voluntary surrender of itself to the common will. And when Peter says, "Honor all men," he is repeating the lesson learned on the house top at Joppa, and saying a broad and difficult thing.

It is a testimony to the lovely unconscious oneness of the Apostolic mind, that St. James, in the fifth Easter Epistle, throws out offhand a wise and glorious phrase about liberty which expresses all that Peter meant. "The perfect law of liberty," says James, and all Wordsworth and Burke, all the brooding of poets and philosophers on the great theme of freedom, is implicit in the words. Both fourth and fifth Epistles are from this most practical of the apostles. But in his own matter-of-fact way, James is as mystical as John. Very sensibly, almost cannily, he exhorts us to be swift to hear and slow to speak, to keep our tempers and our decencies, and to prove our faith by doing good. The fifth Epistle ends with his famous definition of religion in terms of social service, which reads like a motto for a modern school of philanthropy. And all the while he knows that the good gift of our power to behave properly is from above, from the very Father of Lights.

Yes, our feet are on the ground. Life is not any more romantic nor any easier because Christ has risen and our affection is set on things above. Nor, in one sense, is life especially happy. The tone of these Easter epistles is militant and severe: in strange contrast, when one thinks of it, to the general sentiment of the season.

Easter is a Festival for all the world. To many people it means the confused joy of Spring sunshine, bulbs piercing the soil with their green swords, delicate raiment, and release,—not from the Lenten fast, but from an uneasy sense that fasting may be going on somewhere. A jumble of associations,—rabbits, chickens and eggs among them,—is brought to memory by the sacred season.

The Church does not mind. She welcomes everybody to the kind of innocent joy of which he is capable, and hopes that some ray of higher light shines through the most trivial and ephemeral pleasures, and the most cheap and facile sentiment. But for her own, she speaks a different language, harsh to the ear. It is no easy thing to realize eternal life, in time. There is the world to overcome,—and in it we "shall have tribulation"; for antithesis between the world and those who share the Risen Life is taken for granted. We shall weep and lament; we shall suffer wrongfully from our conscience toward God. No smooth prosperity, no facile conforming to current standards, is consonant with the Easter Peace.

For He Who says "Peace be unto you," He Who is ever beside us in His tenderness and His might, bears the wounds of the Passion in Hands and Feet and Side. Out of the great anguish of the ages comes the revelation of the Eternal, and only those who share the anguish can share the Easter joy · "Ye are dead," says the apostle with terrible plainness at the outset of the season. Dead,—dead,—the word recurs. The lower nature, the members that are upon the earth are to be "mortified,"—a fearful phrase, of supreme significance,—by those whose life is hid with Christ in God. Only if the wicked passions which surge upward from our earthiness are buried, putrefied into nothing, by the power of the Christ Arisen, can we ever escape them.

"Hail, Queen Wisdom," says the Poverello of Assisi: "May the Lord save thee with thy sister holy pure Simplicity! O Lady, holy Poverty, may the Lord save thee with thy sister holy Humility!   O all ye most holy virtues, may the Lord from Whom you proceed and come, save you! There is absolutely no man in the whole world who can possess one among you, unless he first die." [1]

When will states as well as persons learn the lesson?

All the time in the Easter Gospels we are hearing marvellous things, unbelievable things: the episodes of the Lord's Appearance, and His most precious words to His own. How He is the Good Shepherd, how He promises the joy no man can

[1] Writings of St. Francis: Fr. Paschal Robinson, p. 78.

take away, how He bids us be of good cheer because He has overcome the world. And always deeper, clearer, sounds the note of promise. Revelation is not closed; the Spirit shall be given, and He when He comes shall teach us all things, and shall reprove the world of sin, of righteousness and of judgment. Only if we heed the straightforward morals of the Epistles have we any right to claim the joy of the Risen Christ or the promise of the Comforter.

Are there any further direct social implications to the Easter teaching?

Of a surety. For if we really believed in Immortality, we should reconstruct all our social values. And if men have always needed real belief they need it supremely now. The contemplation of death has been forced on them as never perhaps before. There should be power in that contemplation to lift classes as well as individuals quite out of those two sins, self-indulgence and greed, which plunged the world into its misery. We dedicate ourselves anew to the ends for which our youth have died.

And to that Other World which is so strangely and suddenly populous, thought is irresistibly drawn. Surely, those objects for which men laid down earthly life are dear to them still. One can not conceive them slipping into a ready-made heaven. Our conception of a life to come must escape everything static or passive; it must adjust itself to a state in which many handicaps are doubtless removed, but in which effort to express love through ever-perfected forms must progress vividly forever. Real belief in a heavenly Commonwealth with real people in it would mean a tremendous deal to life here, and the opening of our twentieth century vision toward the Eternal must help us who are of the "one family, beneath, above," to play our part like men.

But though the war-crisis has accentuated the need of faith, it has not created the need. Immortality is the creed of social hope, and in this light many beside Christian writers have viewed it. Dr. Hyslop, for instance, late secretary of the American Society for Psychical Research, has an interesting passage in his book, *Life After Death*·

"The belief in survival reconciles the imperative of conscience with the limitations under which the fulfilment of it can be attained in this life. Survival gives us time. . . . Immortality is a pivotal belief; that is, supporting in some way a number of other beliefs or maxims of life and conduct. Besides an influence on the individual life,

it has also a great significance for social ethics.
The interest in it may be largely an egoistic one.
It is not always so, for I often meet with those
who care little for it for themselves, but they passionately desire it for their friends or those they
love. It thus becomes an altruistic instinct. . . .
Its ethical implications do not stop with individual
interest. Survival establishes that view of personality which enables us to concentrate emphasis
on the rights of others in the struggle for existence. On the materialistic theory . . . the individual would be tempted to sacrifice all other
personality to his own. But once establish the
fact that personality is permanent, and we have
the eternal value of our neighbor fixed upon as
secure a basis as our own. Man need not stop
with the pursuit of self-interest, but will find his
salvation in the social affections precisely as
taught in primitive Christianity. . . . It is not
that we can directly infer the system of social
ethics from survival or the permanence of personality, but that we can more easily connect this
ethics with a stable basis and reinforce them
[sic!] by the fact of that permanence. The
brotherhood of man will have a new sanction, one
of the sanctions it received in its earlier association in Christianity with the immortality of the

soul. Its natural synthesis is that association.''[1]

Strong testimony, this, against the patronizing assertion, widely current in Victorian times, that the desire for life beyond the grave is fathered by human egotism as it is mothered by human delusion. The ''altruistic instinct,'' as Dr. Hyslop calls it, has been immensely enhanced of late. How about men who do not die by violence, but live out their allotted span on dull and barren levels: the throngs imprisoned, by our stupidity rather than our cruelty, in labor which brings no refreshment and conditions which allow no growth? How about all lives thwarted and suppressed? When the soul shows no prick of life above the earthly surface, as happens often enough irrespective of class or circumstance, the theory of conditional immortality may suffice; but how about the many who would live beautifully if they had a chance, and to whom that chance is denied? In the future of our dreams, that will not happen; but the good life to come will not help the throngs who lived before we learned to set men free,—slaves in ancient Egypt, serfs in mediæval days, modern wage-slaves, victims of family tyranny, the victims everywhere.

Undoubtedly, there was a time when belief in

[1] Life After Death: James H. Hyslop, Ch. XI. E. P. Dutton, 1918.

immortality was dangerous. During the middle ages it probably served as a sedative, and may well have been at times more or less deliberately encouraged for that purpose by the ruling classes, as some modern radicals insist. For the most part, however, the reaction was doubtless unconscious. Oppressors and oppressed alike were inclined to sink back into lazy acquiescence in life's injustice—the former content with the present hour, the latter looking for heavenly compensation: and the revulsion against religion which marked the social revolt of the last century may be traced in part to the scorn this tendency inspired. In the waning twilight of faith in life eternal grew a new passion for justice on earth. Shade is good for little plants; but today that passion has struck roots too deep to be imperilled, and it can be trusted in the sun.

Still, in the fiercely earnest propaganda which goes on among the proletariat, one hears the old cry: that the Church deludes men with insubstantial promises of future bliss, to cut the nerve of effort and of self-defense. And a larger proportion than we realize of the anti-clerical bitterness which pervades the socialist movement may spring from this exasperated conviction. Even philosophic writers insist that Christianity is a servile morality, adapted for the consolation of slaves rather than for the inspiration of strong men. But Christian radicals scout the idea. They know that faith in immortality is in truth now as it was in the beginning, "the sanction for the brotherhood of .man." Our hands are set to build Jerusalem on earth, and as we slowly drag stone on stone, while the generations to our sorrow wait still disherited without the gates of that free city, it is right to lift our hearts for incentive, fortitude and comfort, to that Jerusalem which is Above, where there shall be no decay, no leading into captivity and no complaining in the streets, where happy citizens shall rejoice in fullness of life and health and in such honorable furtherance of all noble ends as only dreams can now foreshadow.

"A lovely city in a lovely land,
  Whose citizens are lovely, and whose king
  Is very Love; to whom all angels sing,

  To whom all saints sing crowned, their sacred
      band
  Saluting Love with palm branch in their hand.
  And thither thou, beloved, and thither I
  May set our heart and set our face and go
  Faint yet pursuing, home on tireless feet." [1]

[1] Christina Rossetti.

Such thoughts, however, legitimate and helpful though they be, are not dwelt upon by the Church in the appointed Scriptures. These, as has been said, keep us strictly to earth, at her homeliest and most difficult. The Risen Lord, with the marks of His Passion on Him, moves among His own in the old scenes, in the familiar ways. As they tread dusty roads, as they eat their suppers, as they ply their trades; in rooms where they were wont to gather, or by the lake whose waters have known the tread of His holy Feet, suddenly He is with them. And what He has to say is what He had said long ago, what He is saying still. Concerning the intercourse of those Forty Days only brief hints are given; but one subject is clearly singled out as the chief theme of the talk: He was with them, "speaking of the things pertaining to the Kingdom of God."

This is really just what we should expect, seeing that the establishment of the Kingdom had been His chief concern during His ministry. In all probability, none of our dominant purposes will be effaced by death; or if they be such that they must perish with the body, we shall be quite literally lost souls in the other world. Jesus, having passed through the grave and gate of that great experience, is still bent as ever on training his followers to create the Beloved Community. The bitterness of Gethsemane had been that He seemed frustrated in that work. Perfect Humanity had to know frustration, otherwise Christ could not have been our Brother; but the will "in-oned" with God's Will is never defeated, and His will proved to be God's Will after all.

Probably they would rather have had Him talk of something else. They were reverent Jews, and they had walked some time with Jesus, so that what we call the supernatural would have been taken by them more quietly than by us. That He whom they loved was with them again, doubtless filled their hearts and minds. At the same time, being human, they must have longed to ask Him a hundred questions about those mysteries beyond the veil which the human heart down the ages so longs to fathom. But He did not talk to them about Paradise,—the Penitent Thief knew more about that than St. John was allowed to know. He talked about the Kingdom of God, the blessed fellowship, the ideal society, which from the day He first spoke in a Galilean synagogue had been the burden of His teaching. We associate the teaching of the Kingdom with the bright times of the early ministry, and easily forget that it belongs just as much to these last mystical phases of Christ's intercourse with His disciples. Yet it does. This is the purpose He entrusts to them, this the Gospel which they are to carry to the uttermost ends of the earth.

Just what was said in these conversations of the Master with His happy friends, we do not know. They were conversations, not dialogues, for the most part. Once in a while, a blessed person sees Him alone: Peter; the Magdalen; and, surely, though Holy Writ knows naught of it, His mother. But the group life goes on, and it is in and through the group that He is working.

Some people think that He is telling the apostles how to organize the Church. Possibly; we like to sing:

> "I love Thy Kingdom, Lord,
> The house of Thine abode,
> The Church our blessed Redeemer saved
> With His own precious blood."

And the ecclesiastical definition has been current from early times. But there is scant basis for it in the Bible, and the idea of the Kingdom is belittled when confined to the imperfect and partial expression, in the Church visible, militant here below. The Church is doubtless the natural, the appointed instrument of the Kingdom, but it would take an inveterate optimism to identify the two.

The "dear truth" of the Kingdom was to the Jews, as we have already seen, the hope of a holy society here on earth of which Messiah should be king. Probably before the Passion the disciples had not risen above a national patriotism; the Kingdom was to be exclusively for their own suffering race. But the Master had been busy replacing the nationalistic by the social conception, always tacitly, at times explicitly; nor can it be doubted that it was the social conception which He now sought to establish in those hearts who, filled with Resurrection joy, listened to the Voice of the Beloved. He imparted no elaborate theology, hardening experience into dogma; that task was left for His followers to accomplish under the Spirit's guidance as the ages went on. What He gave them to transmit was the old Gospel, the Good News, the glad tidings, preached first of all to the poor, which from the first ran through His teachings like a golden thread, binding all portions of it together.

What that Resurrection teaching meant to the Apostles, we can know only imperfectly. They were ordinary men, bound by their race and their age. The Book of Acts and the Epistles do not use often the phrase, The Kingdom of God. It is not a Pauline expression; to the apostle to the Gentiles, it has already been merged in the conception of the Church. During the long course of Christian history from apostolic days till now, the full force of the conception of Jesus has been systematically neglected and sadly missed. But modern study stimulates us to a deeper comprehension and a loyalty renewed.

We know that Jesus meant the Kingdom to reverse the laws of unregenerate society, giving all blessedness of earth and heaven to the poor, the merciful, the anhungered for justice, the peace-makers, the meek, the pure in heart,—thus releasing the creative and discrediting the possessive instincts; we know that its laws were conceived as operative in a fellowship, wherein all normal joys and ties were sanctioned, while all that savored of separation and selfishness was to be purged away. And it is evident that the Lord thought of this fellowship of His citizens as bound to higher allegiance than that to any worldly power, and therefore sure to find its true blessedness through persecution; and that He was quietly assured that of this Kingdom he Himself was king, and that the last stage of it was to be inaugurated by His coming to judge the world. These great ideas in their plenitude were probably the burden of His discourse during the Forty Days; on this social vision of an ideal community, the Risen Lord fixes the gaze of His own.

Detroit, martyrdom — true goal/model for all Xian living

So the Church reaches her Ascension-Tide and the consummation of the earthly story. The disciples are at their old tricks again. "Lord," they ask Him, "wilt thou at this time restore again the kingdom—*to Israel?*" He is, as ever, fulfilled in patience. While they could still think in narrow terms like these, He knows that preparation is not complete; they do not possess the needed power. But He is also fulfilled in hope and faith, and so He answers: "It is not for you to know the times or the seasons. . . . But ye shall receive power after the Holy Ghost is come upon you."

That in these last moments, He persistently stresses the larger thought, is evident in both the Epistle and the Gospel for Ascension Day. In the Gospel, the Great Commission is given: not to Israel alone, but "Go ye into *all the world,* and preach the Gospel"—the Glad Tidings of the Kingdom of God, "to every creature." In the "Epistle," He says that they are to be witnesses to Him, not only in Judæa, not only in Samaria even, but "unto the uttermost parts of the earth." It is on these words that He leaves them; words spoken, a suggestive old legend says, as He ascends, His sight embracing wider and wider reaches of the landscape. At all events His spirit ever beheld regions beyond their narrow vision.

They are left gazing upward; and two men in white apparel bring once more at this solemn moment the promise of His return. The lesson is for us as for those of old. As Heaven stoops to earth so earth must attain to Heaven till there is no more near nor far. We must in heart and mind thither ascend and with Christ continually dwell. Yet earth may not be forgotten. Still, as ever, the gaze of the Christian is pointed forward by the Heavenly messengers, and what shall happen here, not what goes on behind the veil of death, is the goal of Christian hope.

We wait, with the apostles, the promised Spirit. There is an old Greek prayer for Ascension-Tide, which takes more interest in the state of things here below than does our own Collect, translated from the Sarum antiphon: "O Thou Who art ascended to the heavens, whence Thou didst descend, Lord, leave us not orphans"—so far the prayer is like our own—"Let Thy Spirit, *bringing peace to the world,* come and manifest the works of Thy power, O merciful Lord, to the sons of men."

The Epistle for the Sunday after Ascension Day reminds us once again. The end of all things is at hand, says Peter: watch therefore, watch, and love, and show your love by sharing one with another. We have been bad enough at loving,

God knows but even a little worse, perhaps, at watching. The Gospel strikes again the note of the persecution, to be surely expected by all true witnesses of Christ: persecution, not by wicked people, be it noted, but by the respectable and the godly: "They shall put you out of the synagogues; yea, the time cometh that whosoever killeth you will think that he doeth God service." There is much in these solemn warnings, deliberately incorporated by the Church in her most sacred days, that ordinary Christians can not by any stretch of application appropriate to themselves!

But the Comforter, the Spirit of Truth Who shall bring all things to our remembrance, is promised; and year by year the Church waits with the disciples in the Upper Chamber, confident that the best is yet to be and that she shall receive the promised Power.

CHAPTER VIII: WHITSUNTIDE

Antiphon: How hear we every man in our own tongue, wherein we were born?

V. They began to speak with other tongues,

R. As the Spirit gave them utterance.

O God, Who as at this time didst teach the hearts of Thy faithful people, by sending to them the light of Thy Holy Spirit; Grant us by the same Spirit to have a right judgment in all things, and evermore to rejoice in His holy comfort; through the merits of Christ Jesus our Saviour, Who liveth and reigneth with Thee, in the unity of the same Spirit, one God, world without end.   Amen.

GOD among us, our Brother,—that has been the centre of thought from Advent until now. God within us, our Indweller,—to this deepest sanctuary of experience, we are summoned by Whitsunday.

This faith in the Indwelling Spirit is the final sanction and seal of democracy. Lacking it, most thinking people would automatically become aristocrats:

> "Thou art a man: God is no more:
> Thy own humanity learn to adore,"[1]

cries William Blake. But belief in humanity as even potentially divine, is the last triumphant defiance to the aspect of things,—a defiance very difficult to sustain in the face of the sorrowful human story. To know that God created us is scant comfort; it but deepens our shame as we see "what man has made of man." To know that God becomes Man and suffers with man is indeed

[1] Blake: The Everlasting Gospel.

the source of strength and consolation; yet one can not forget the daily spectacle, patent to seeing eyes, of man crucifying the God who saves him. But He Who is the Eternal Seeker, the insatiate Lover, has further reassurance to offer our despair. He comes as the Paraclete, the Comforter, the sweet Guest of the Soul, a guest whom no sin of ours can exile. The heavenly spark is part of our existence; it is the spark of life without which the soul were not. He Who is Creator and Redeemer is also Sanctifier, and our very being, broken and desecrated though it be, is the Temple of His Presence.

There is a definite reason for the certain fact that in the modern world, immanential ideas have accompanied the rise of democracy. As the People have been coming to their own, the visible emblems of King or Judge or even of Father, which had sufficed monarchical and autocratic times, as all religious art can testify, have lost reality. They have been replaced more and more by a burning intuition of a Presence, closer than breathing, nearer than hands and feet. The Christian must claim as his own the splendid passages inspired by the vibrating recognition of Universal Spirit, which are the culminating glory of early nineteenth century poetry in England:

"I have felt
A Presence that disturbs me with the joy
Of elevated thoughts; a sense sublime
Of something far more deeply interfused,
Whose dwelling is the light of setting suns,
And the round ocean, and the living air,
And the blue sky, and in the mind of man:
A motion and a spirit, that impels
All living things, all objects of all thought,
And rolls through all things."[1]

"The One Spirit's plastic stress
Sweeps through the dull dense world, compelling
there
All new successions to the forms they wear;
Torturing th' unwilling dross that checks its flight
To its own likeness, as each mass may bear;
And bursting in its beauty and its might
From trees and beasts and men into the Heaven's
light."[2]

The Christian feels that all phases of religious
intuition are included within the grand scope of
the Catholic faith; and the pantheism of modern
poets and philosophers, from Blake to Whitman

[1] Wordsworth: Lines composed a few miles above Tintern
Abbey.
[2] Shelley: Adonais, XLIII.

and beyond, is to his mind an impressive witness to the truth reiterated Sunday by Sunday in our Confession: our faith in "the Lord, and Giver of Life," the "Creator Spirit by Whose aid the world's foundations first were laid."

True, Christian thought has always shrunk from pantheism, fearing, and rightly, its tendency to blur moral distinctions, and to sink back into ultimate fatalism. The latter tendency has not been marked perhaps in the Western world; the former is obvious, in the whole modern movement of revolt which sweeps democracy along in its current. But the Church finds protection from this danger through the insistence with which she places the doctrine of the Spirit last instead of first, in the unfolding conception of deity. The great sequence cost her a tremendous struggle to guard, but it is established for all time in the faith of the Western Church; and the Procession of the Spirit from the Son protects the dignity and primacy of human character, and robs pantheistic ideals of all their danger. Since the Informing Spirit Who is the soul of the world, flows forth from Him Who was made Man, as well as from the ultimate perfection of the Divine Fatherhood, our reverence for our own moral nature and our aspiration toward endless progress are alike assured.

This Spirit, Who brooded at the outset over the
face of the waters, Whose life is the sustaining life
of Nature and of man, is the very Spirit of Pentecost. But in a new and special sense, ''the soul's
most welcome Guest'' visits the waiting disciples
of Jesus:

''Witness, O Church, with whom His promised
    Spirit
Dwells through the ages, His ever-gracious Will.''

Whitsunday is the birthday of the Church: and
the Church is to be the instrument of that democracy through which the Indwelling Spirit is to
work out His blessed will.

Instrument of democracy? One hears the answering sneer. But the Church has been true to
her duty in more ways than the scoffer allows,
though often, as must be granted, without the
knowledge or even against the will of her living
officials. At the outset of life, she assures the
Gift of the Spirit to her children through Baptism, which is the very sacrament of equality.
''The first thing the Church has to do is, in the
face of competing sects and classes, to bear witness to the essential equality of the whole people.
This she does by means of her Sacrament of
Infant Baptism. Every little human being born

into London is claimed as being the equal of every other little human being."[1] The Eucharist which feeds the faithful is the sign and seal of brotherhood; and the Scriptures which the Church so jealously guards are the charter of freedom.

Liberty, equality, fraternity! Charles Kingsley once aroused the wrath of a mid-Victorian clergyman. "The Church," said Kingsley, "has three special possessions and treasures: the Bible, which proclaims man's freedom; baptism, his equality; the Lord's Supper, his brotherhood." The incumbent of the parish was so horrified at this incendiary statement that he rose after the sermon and denounced his guest; but Kingsley spoke sober truth.

Nor are sacraments or Scriptures empty symbols of truth forgotten or denied. The Church has held to her democratic purpose, often unconsciously, to be sure, but always, beneath the surface, steadfastly. Sometimes, it must be granted, her witness has been borne almost in spite of her intentions. The mediæval Church, for example, inspired by a powerful conviction of her superiority to the external order, tried to overtop that order in magnificence and in autocratic assumptions; her very hierarchy reproduced the

[1]Stewart Headlam: A Lent in London, p. 127.

feudal model, and seemed remote enough from the plain fishermen of Galilee. Yet at the same time, within her own borders she fostered democracy to a surprising degree. Peasant and noble were alike eligible to her highest honors, and her saints were drawn from every rank. Monastic life, even at its average, nay even in its decadence, somewhat resembled a communist Utopia colored by asceticism. The supreme importance of every least and meanest soul was matter of absolute faith to the haughtiest monarch, and such faith was perpetually at work, modifying the prevalent caste-ideal.

Open confession is good for the soul. The Church has been guilty, as her accusers claim, of systematic exploitation, of worldiness and arrogance; she has committed almost fatal blunders, from the evil day when she accepted the Gift of Constantine to her endorsement of the *ancien régime* at the close of the eighteenth century. There is danger that she will repeat these blunders in our own day; free and established Churches alike have shown of late a tendency to come to heel like obedient dogs at the whistle of the State, and the situation in Russia is disquieting and obscure. Nevertheless, she has never

Today churches aligning w/ political parties —
#1 - "Abortion", #2 Family

wholly forfeited her proud dignity of being the refuge of the humble, the home of the One Family of God.

But it is more consoling, and frankly easier also, to follow the lead and teaching of the Prayer-Book than to proffer an Apologia for the Church in history. And the Prayer-Book leads us straight to the Upper Chamber, where the little group quietly awaits the Promise of the Lord.

Great events often happen unobtrusively, in out of the way corners of the world. It is not at all likely that any one in Italy or Africa or Greece or Asia had the least idea on that Sunday morning that something momentous was going on in a modest upstairs room of a provincial capital, where a group of working-folk was gathered. Yet nothing else of comparable importance was occurring anywhere else in the world.

The Gift, like all best gifts, was not given in solitude. John and Peter each knew that the same wonderful thing was happening to his friend.

"Not on one favored forehead fell
    Of old the fire-tongued miracle,
    But flamed o'er all the thronging host
    The baptism of the Holy Ghost;

Heart answers heart; in one desire
The blending lines of prayer aspire." [1]

And from that day to this, the Spirit is sacramentally given where two or three are met. Those outside the old historic tradition of Christendom resent the Catholic custom of associating the Gift of the Spirit with human agency,—the claim, almost if not quite from the Day of Pentecost on, to transmit the Gift at confirmation and ordination by the touch of fatherly hands. Yet the custom and the claim speak steadfastly of the fact that not in isolation but in fellowship is found the deepest contact with the Divine. The consecrated touch, transmitted through the ages, is the silent witness of the Church to the union of humanity in God. Even hermit-priests, who fled into the desert or otherwise separated themselves from men, had known that touch; they were one with the family of God. Those lonely souls who prefer to depend solely on the visitation of the Breath in solitude, turn from the method of Christ, and forfeit surely something of His Blessing.

So were they all with one accord in one place,—gathered from the world, not because they were more holy but because they knew a greater love.

[1] John Whittier.

So came to them the mystic Wind, the mystic Flame; the cloven tongues descend, and the undivided Fire,—note the use of the singular,—sits upon each of them.

And the first sign of the Spirit is the Gift of Tongues. The Beloved Community receives the heavenly power, but it may not for the briefest period keep its blessing to itself. Instantly, the disciples "began to speak with other tongues, as the Spirit gave them utterance." It was to the multitude they spoke, "devout men of every nation under heaven," and, at least in the early days, there was no incomprehensible gibberish in that speaking· "Behold, are not all these which speak Galileans? And how hear we every man in our own tongue, wherein we were born, Parthians, and Medes, and Elamites,—Jews and proselytes, Cretes and Arabians, we do hear them speak in our tongues the wonderful works of God." The first purpose of the Gift of Tongues was that every stranger and alien should understand God's Revelation.

Perhaps this power to make oneself more widely understood is always the first result of true illumination by the Holy Spirit. But it is a power to which men appear sadly indifferent. How many people in Germany were able during the war to speak with the tongues that could be understood of Frenchmen? How many Americans are praying for the grace of the Spirit to enable them to declare in language intelligible to the German or the Russian mind, the wonderful works of God?

The Gift of Tongues, the Gift of Sympathy! The ability to make oneself understood, not by forcing or even urging other people to learn our language, but by talking to them in their own. Whether we look at the corporate Church or at our private behavior, it seems equally forgotten that this is what the Spirit must do for us. As a rule, the idea is twisted completely round. Every man and every class is content to shout its shibboleth at its adversary, hoping to convince him by deafening him. So capital addresses labor, so labor capital; so even the Christian Church tries to coax the unchurched to come and learn her ways and speak her tongue, rarely indeed trying the other way. How much authentic effort is made by Slav, Saxon, Latin to understand each other? Lacking an international psychology, how can a League of Nations flourish? How many people take the trouble to ascertain what the Bolsheviki are really doing? . . . In this "Pentecost of Calamity," the whole world seems given over to a chaos of misrepresentation and misunderstanding, a clash of tongues not holy,

rising from every newspaper, dinner-table, public
meeting,—drowning the clear under-melody, constant for who can hear, of the Secret Guest of the
Soul,—the One Spirit Whose undivided life we
share. And every man thinking that it is the
other man's fault,—that the antagonist ought to
take the trouble to learn *his* language. As for
the personal application   as between mistress
and servant, employer and employed, old and
young . . . Spirit of Pentecost, grant us the Gift
of Tongues, whereby each man shall understand
the language of the other! *Charlotte*

But if we would have this Gift, the suggestion
of the Whitsunday Epistle is, that we must be
speaking of the wonderful works of God.

That is what the Apostles did. Peter's sermon,
spoken while the flame hovered almost visibly
above him (the first sermon ever preached by the
Christian Church), carried the democratic message: "To you is the promise and to your children, *and to all that are afar off*, even as many as
the Lord our God shall call unto Him." On Whitsun Monday, the Church reads to us another
sermon of Peter's, where he says that God is no
respecter of persons, but that in every nation
he that feareth him and worketh righteousness is
accepted. Such teaching as this did not come easy
to nationalistic Peter; he had to be taught by

vision and miracle that his Jewish exclusiveness
is played out and that there is nothing common
or unclean. Even so, he went right on opposing
Paul and insisting on the circumcision. Yet while
he preached those sermons, under the power of
the Baptism of Fire, he knew true "sight of
soul"; and the Holy Ghost fell on the Gentiles as
well as on the Jews, to the astonishment of the
latter, and Peter rose to the occasion, saying,
"Can any man forbid water, that these should
not be baptized which have received the Holy
Ghost as well as we?"

On Whitsun Tuesday, we hear how fellowship
reaches out into Samaria. An amazing thing,
for the Jews, in the Gospels, have no dealings with
the Samaritans. But now Peter and John are
sent into those parts by the Apostolic College,
and the Samaritans, who had already, it seems,
heard the Word and been baptized, received the
Spirit by the laying on of hands. Thus the Beloved Community becomes more than a special
union of those who have been extraordinarily
blessed at a crisis; it is established on secure foundations, on which down all ages it shall endure.

So the birthday of the Church is the birthday of
Internationalism. At Whitsuntide, the Church
summons the faithful to advance into Christian
history, beyond the brief period when the Light

shone and the Life was manifest in Galilee and Jerusalem. And the history of early Christianity as recorded in the Book of Acts and the Epistles, is largely the story of the struggle between a nationalistic and an international ideal. The latter triumphed, and the primitive Church became in a surprisingly short time an international institution. Today, a divided Christendom sorrowfully attests how difficult it is to maintain the great vision; yet the wonderful sense of expanding and all-inclusive life which pervades the Whitsun season, remains the Christian temper *par excellence.*

The first result then of this influx of the Spirit is the breaking down of barriers, the creation of a limitless democracy in Christ. And the next is the development of simple social organization in the new community. The first and most distinctive mark of it, as recorded in Scripture, is the community of goods. "And not one of them said that aught of the things which he possessed was his own; but they had all things common. And with great power gave the apostles their witness of the Resurrection of the Lord Jesus: and great grace was upon them all. For neither was there among them any that lacked: for as many as were possessors of lands or houses, sold them, and brought the prices of the things that were sold, and laid them at the apostles' feet: and distribution was made unto each according as any one had need."[1]

One would not make too much of that brief experiment at Jerusalem. It should indeed be called experience rather than experiment, since there was in it no self-conscious playing with possibilities, but merely the straight instinctive expression of the new-found unity in the Risen Lord. That short-lived episode of brotherhood did not start from a well considered economic theory; it just happened. Men poured all that they had into the common stock because they loved one another so much that they enjoyed sharing better than keeping. The method was abandoned presently, even in New Testament days: the poor saints at Jerusalem proved, it must be confessed, rather a nuisance and problem to the rest of the Christian world. In the centuries after Church life became crystallized, orthodox opinion on average levels has considered, when it discussed economic ideals at all, that communism is a sort of counsel of perfection, to be relegated to the New Jerusalem or to monastic orders (among which it has parenthetically shown itself marvellously potent to release and fructify men's capacities). Scholars

[1] Acts IV, 32-35. See also Acts II, 44-46.

tell us that even those first disciples, at that moment of heightened emotion, adopted the method only as an *ad interim* policy, because the Messiah was expected to return any day, and there was therefore no especial object in hoarding wealth. Nor were any orders issued on the matter: the resigning one's goods was a voluntary measure, untouched by taint of legislation. The trouble with Ananias, as has often been pointed out, was not that he kept part of his possessions back, but that he lied about them.

Yet when all modifications and admissions are made, the Christian mind can never forget those brief days, marked by the first outflowing of the Spirit into a Christian commonwealth. President Faunce put the situation well:

"They had all things common,—not only a common faith and hope and zeal, but common property also. Within the Church of Jerusalem, private property largely disappeared, and community of goods was the rule. The early Church was not only a prayer-meeting but a mutual benefit association. Its members were not only 'saved from the wrath,' but they were insured against poverty and sickness by the organization which they joined. There was a share of possessions as well as ideals. The first official action after Pentecost was the choice of seven men 'over this business,'—the intelligent care of the poor. Organized relief of poverty in Jerusalem preceded all attempts at the formulation of Christian truth." [1]

Such is the first Adventure of the Church, fresh from her chrism of Pentecostal fire. It is not by chance that the incident occurred or that it is recorded. The meaning, at lowest, is that the Holy Ghost leads the Church straight to distinctive self-expression concerning worldly wealth and social relationships, and that the right attitude toward property is a primary object of Christian solicitude. It is natural, then, at this season, to glance at successive phases of Christian thinking in this connection, and to note how the instinct of ownership, so potent and to most minds so essential a social force, is consistently discredited to the best Christian intuition. The idea of literal communism yields almost at once indeed under stress of actuality, to the cognate yet quite separate theory of stewardship; but this theory, though it may easily become a means of self-delusion, is taken by all great Christian writers with such literal seriousness that it would involve practical renunciation of all special privilege. Nor is it too much to say that the more intense

[1] W. H. P. Faunce: Social Aspects of Foreign Missions, p. 20. Missionary Education Movement, 1914.

the spiritual note, the more the key of pure communism is struck.

"It was largely because the Church appeared as a society making the welfare of all its members its controlling principle in the acquisition and distribution of wealth that it made the great progress which history records in the world of the Roman Empire." So states the Report of a Commission to the Convocation of Canterbury in 1907. A good summary of the early attitude is found in a volume introduced by Bishop Gore, "Property, Its Duties and Rights": What has religion to say to the institution of Property? "The (early) Christian Church became a corporation for mutual support, refusing the idler who would not work, but for the rest accepting the maxim that they 'must provide one another with support, with all joy. . . . To the workman, work; to him who can not work, mercy (or alms).' There is no doubt that this profound sense of the communal claim on private property, and this practically effective sense of brotherhood produced an economic condition in the Christian community which was one main cause of its progress."[1] (The internal quotation is from the eighth Epistle of the Pseudo-Clement.)

---

[1] Property, Its Duties and Rights. Macmillan, 1913. Introduction, p. xv. A valuable book.

From the same book comes a summary of the attitude of Lactantius, a third-century writer especially concerned with social speculation:

"God . . . has willed that all should be equal, that is, equally matched (*pares*). None is with Him a slave, none a master. . . . Wherefore neither the Romans nor the Greeks could possess justice, because they have had men of many unequal grades, from poor to rich, from humble to powerful. For where all are not equally matched, there is not equity; and *inequality itself excludes justice*." [1] A startling statement, worthy of Lenin!

Another epitome: "Clement can find no Christian warrant for the man who 'goes on trying to increase without limit.' On the other hand, he goes beyond the primitive mode of thought in a modern direction when he observes that 'It is impossible that one in want of the necessaries of life should not be harassed in mind and lack leisure for the better things.' . . . In Tertullian the primitive attitude toward property is no less manifest than in his great Alexandrine contemporary. 'We who mingle in mind and soul,' says he, 'have no hesitation as to fellowship in property.' " [2]

[1] Ditto, p. 105.
[2] Ditto, pp. 102, 103.

From the Epistle of Barnabas: "Thou shalt communicate in all things with thy neighbor; thou shalt not call things thine own; for if ye are partakers of things which are incorruptible, how much more of those things which are corruptible."

"Thou dost not give to the poor what is thine own, thou restorest to him what is his. The earth belongs to all, not to the rich only. Thou art there for paying thy debt, and givest him only what thou owest him." That is St. Ambrose.

And St. Augustine: "Let us then, my brethren, abstain from private property, or at least from the love of it, if we can not abstain from its possession." And again: "All that God has given us beyond what is necessary He has not, properly speaking, given us. He has but entrusted it to us, that it may by our means come into the hands of the poor. To retain it is to take possession of what belongs to others."

St. Chrysostom is a particularly radical-minded Father. One could fill pages with quotations from him:

"So destructive a passion is avarice that to grow rich without injustice is impossible. . . . Because God in the beginning made not one man rich and another poor, . . . but He left the earth free to all alike. Why, then, if it is common, have you so many acres of land, and your neighbor has not a portion of it?"

He is quite aware, however, that the day of the apostolic Christians is over, and indulges in a delightful note of satire·

"They did not give in part and in part reserve; nor yet in giving all, give it as their own. And they lived, moreover, in great abundance," a remark hardly justified by the record; "they removed all inequality from among them and made a goodly order. . . . To" the apostles "they left" it to be the dispensers, made them the owners, that henceforth all should be defrayed as from common not from private property. . . . Let us now depict this state of things in words, and derive at least this pleasure from it, since you have no mind for it in your actions."

I do not know who wrote the Tenth Homily, on the First Epistle to the Corinthians, but he was a perfect Bolshevik:

"Your very existence is not your own: how is it then that your riches are? . . . Riches are a common property, like the light of the sun, the air or the productions of the earth. Riches are to society what food is to the body: should any one of her members wish to absorb the nutriment which is intended for the support of all, the body would perish entirely: it is held together only by the requisite distribution of nourishment to diverse parts."[1]

None of these early writers anticipate or urge the expression of their generous ideals in the secular structure; the antithesis between the faithful and "the world" was sharp and permanent to their minds: only the Power of the Spirit could inspire fraternal passion to inhibit the possessive instincts of the natural man. But they thought the motives at work in the world frankly evil; nor could they have encountered without surprise or discussed with patience the modern Apologia for competition, inequalities of wealth, and private ownership, on the ground that such things are morally to the good.

As the generations passed, the disparity between the Christians and the world softened in fact, though never abandoned in theory. After the Gift of Constantine, the present situation soon defined itself: "a diffusion of Christianity at the cost of its intensity." The mediæval Church, with its pomp, its vast endowments, and the overweening luxury of its prelates, presented a sharp external contrast to earlier ideals. The private possession of wealth was not discouraged, since a

[1] See, for further extracts from Church Fathers, Upton Sinclair, The Cry for Justice, Section, "The Voice of the Early Church," pp. 396-399.

large portion was likely to flow in time into
ecclesiastical coffers. Long after the middle ages
were past, Burke, in famous passages aglow with
a great tradition, exalted with unsurpassed elo-
quence the dignities of material splendor as the
necessary trappings of religion.

And yet through the long middle ages the more
radical attitude toward private wealth was far
from forgotten. It found at once satisfaction and
check in expression on a limited scale. Communism and voluntary poverty might be beyond
the duty of common folk; but they inspired the
great monastic foundations and they were steadily
recognized by theologians as an integral part of
the Christian ideal. It is not necessary to turn
to avowed radicals like the Spiritual Franciscans
to find stubborn reassertion of the vices of private
property; one can listen to St. Thomas Aquinas
saying: "Man should not consider his outward
possessions as his own, but as common to all, so
as to share them without difficulty when others are
in need." The mystics according to their wont
are more explicit than the theologians. Fine passages in the "Theologia Germanica" go to the
heart of the matter:

"Were there no self-will there would be also no
ownership. In Heaven there is no ownership.
. . If anyone there took upon him to call any-

thing his own, he would straightway be thrust out into hell, and would become an evil spirit. . . ." "Now in this present time, man is set between Heaven and hell, and may turn him toward which he will. For the more he hath of ownership, the more he hath of sin and misery." "He who hath something or seeketh or longeth to have something of his own, is himself a slave, and he who hath nothing of his own, nor seeketh nor longeth thereafter, is free and at large and in bondage to none." [1]

The early communism of Wyclif has been too much thrown in the shade by his later theological heresies. But it is a theory definitely thought out, in direct line from Marsiglio of Padua and the Spiritual Franciscans. The arguments in his "De Dominio Civile" are quaint, but the conclusions are both primitive and modern. Briefly, Wyclif thinks that only righteous people have any claim on possessions; but righteous people never want to keep anything to themselves, *ergo* common property is the only just and Christian ideal. In the following passage, he wrestles with a difficulty often urged today:

"It will be objected to holding goods in common that government will perish, because no one cares to preserve common property. But no, if that

[1] Theologia Germanica, Ch. LI.

law were in force states would be most excellently preserved. . . . For goods are to be cared for in proportion to their excellence. Now goods held in common are the best of all; therefore they must be cared for most perfectly.''

The Beatified Sir Thomas More, at the outset of the Reformation, fused his Catholic inheritance with his Platonic studies, and remarked in no uncertain tones that private property was the root of all evil. But when we reach the Reformation, quotations must cease. Despite Anabaptists and other social stirrings such as always accompany religious reform at the outset, Protestantism on the whole grew and flourished in the period of lusty individualism which is just passing away, and socialist theory is weak and occasional. The nineteenth century began to strike the old note once more. Canon Barnett, that true prophet, wrote: ''There will be in the Christian society no governed and governing classes.'' Walter Rauschenbusch more lately uttered an epigrammatic warning: ''If the Kingdom of God is the true human society, it is a fellowship of justice, equality and love. But it is hard to get riches with justice, to keep them with equality, and to spend them with love.''[1] Even the official Church

[1] W. Rauschenbusch: Christianity and the Social Crisis, p. 77. Macmillan.

begins to look back with wistfulness to that first Christian community, fresh from the outpouring of the Spirit; and here and there, a Christian voice is clearly raised with the old message.

Once more, men begin to perceive that the first Pentecostal experiment derived straight from Christ's own Teachings. The Spirit has indeed taken of His and has shown it unto us.

As Bishop Gore says: "Our Lord seems to stand over against each human soul which comes to Him to seek the position of the disciple, eliciting, claiming, welcoming, and blessing, the renunciation of wealth. 'How hardly shall they that have riches enter into the Kingdom of Heaven.' . . . From that warning we must remember the correctest texts have removed the modification, 'How hardly shall they that trust in riches.' It is the possession of riches which remains the almost insuperable obstacle." [1]

Individuals by thousands have heeded the warning. They have seen that Christ invariably stressed worldly prosperity as a perilous though not fatal condition, and they have sought safety, peace and citizenship in the Kingdom of Heaven, by claiming the Beatitude of the Poor. But the segregated methods of monasticism do not satisfy a democratic world, and few see that it would do

[1] Sermon to Church Congress, 1906.

anybody any good for them to follow St. Francis. Individual obedience to the Divine Commands is at best a partial solution; for one can not iterate too often that those commands invariably presuppose a Fellowship and a social application. It is conceivable that a corporate expression of the Christian attitude toward property and private wealth would give Christianity a chance for the first time.

Economic revolution sweeps over the world. While socialism of conservative types cautiously and almost unrecognized makes its way in nearly every country, an amazing experiment in communism, boldly based upon the ultimate communist formulæ, seizes possession of a great nation. Men wait breathless upon the event. In most countries, notably in Russia, the radical movement assumes without discussion that the Church is its settled enemy, and the firm friend of the *ancien régime*. It would be interesting indeed to surprise the Revolution! If Christian people regained the Pentecostal fervor, they might play the determining and the constructive part in these tremendous days. They, and they only, have it in their power to rescue the Revolution from its worst evils. They might, if they would, transfuse the passionate upheaval which is bound to stop nowhere short of the extended socialization of wealth, with the passion of the Cross, with the fire of the Spirit. Does it mean nothing that our Whitsun Altars glow with red? Might not the Red Flag find itself at home there?

The Church is at the parting of the ways; before long she will have to declare herself for or against the socialist movement. She can not remain neutral, because she is composed of human beings. It would be a tragic blunder if she should repeat her successive choices in history, and constitute herself the defender of the economic *status quo*. Modern critical study has given a new actuality to the Teachings of Christ. Is it not a Christian hope that the Church may recover that first ardor which filled those eager disciples at Jerusalem, on whose brows the Spirit still lingered in living flame?

If the Indweller guides her, some of us can not doubt the answer. The overflowing love of God, of which the Whitsun Gospels speak, will inundate her heart, and all jealous separateness in outward possessions as in the inward parts, will be swept away. The Spirit shall bring to our remembrance all things, whatsoever Christ has said unto us, and we shall know the peace that is not of this world. Jesus the Door, Jesus the Shepherd, shall open the way to a new social life of economic equality and shall guide us as we enter in.

CHAPTER IX: TRINITY-TIDE

Antiphon: And they rest not day nor night, saying Holy, Holy, Holy, Lord God Almighty, which was, and is, and is to come.

V. Hallowed be Thy Name,
R. On earth as it is in Heaven.

Almighty and everlasting God, Who hast given unto us Thy servants grace, by the confession of a true faith, to acknowledge the glory of the eternal Trinity, and in the power of the Divine Majesty to worship the Unity; We beseech Thee that Thou wouldest keep us steadfast in this faith, and evermore defend us from all adversities, Who livest and reignest, one God, world without end.   Amen.

CHAPTER IX: TRINITY-TIDE

THE Year of the Church draws to an end. The varying contacts of the Divine with the human celebrated by the seasons as they pass, converge toward their centre and climax,—the contemplation of the Divine Nature, as it exists eternal, self-sufficing, uncreate.

A right conception of God is the greatest need of humanity, and it should be the first object of human desire. That such was the belief of Jesus is made clear by the sequence of petitions in the Lord's Prayer. "Hallowed be Thy Name!" A name is an idea or definition of a person or thing, and the hallowing, that is, the sanctification and exaltation of our idea of God, is to be our first aspiration. This aspiration heads the great group of impersonal requests which, contrary to natural instinct, precede the demands for physical sustenance and even for spiritual well-being.

In no wise is this prayer more truly the Lord's Prayer than in such contradiction. Dear Father in Heaven, give us our daily bread; forgive us our sins, deliver us from evil: our own needs clamor to Thee, and we can not pay attention to anything else till they are satisfied. Then, for we do really and honestly want a better world, may Thy Kingdom come and Thy Will be done on earth. And when all these things are accomplished, perhaps we shall find time to be concerned about our theology, and anxious for the hallowing of Thy Name. . . . That is a familiar type of prayer, not irreligious, much better one fears than the average, and quite in accord with the idea held by some radicals and also some psychologists of the sequence of our needs. Only, it is not the prayer of Our Lord Jesus Christ.

That any human conception of God is final, who would dare to claim? What eternity, or even the future course of history, may reveal, who would dare to prophesy? Peering back to the beginning of racial life, we see man's thought about the Supreme Power continually changing; the very name varies today from country to country, nor can God be etymologically recognized in Dieu, Allah, Jehovah, or Bogh. In one sense, man discovers his God, in another he creates Him; the conception of Deity is always deeply affected, if not produced, by the social and economic conditions of the age.

The Lord is a Man of War: the Lord is His

Name. He was a fetich before that, a dim Anima
Mundi, half-conscious in wood or stone. Among
the ancient nations, one notes confusedly, now the
adoration of life in Nature, now the anthropo-
morphic insistence on a human God, now the
exaltation of culture-heroes. In every age are
philosophic or mystic souls, to whom the veil of
sense is thin, who fly through illusions to the One;
in every age the multitude, with a wisdom of its
own, cries out insistently to the Many. Now a
daze of undifferentiated light, negation rather
than completion of earth's rainbow, invites the
weary spirit of the Buddhist; now the disciple of
Confucius sees nothing higher than the category
of the moral law.

Among the Jews, steady advance can be traced
from the comparatively late stage of belief in a
tribal Deity with which their history opens: and
in due time comes the shining hour when man
utters the word which he will never forget, and
cries Father into the waiting heavens. Our Lord,
in His revelation of the Divine Fatherhood, exalted forever the ideal native to a once patriarchal
people, among whom reverence for family life had
reached a higher point than among any other
people of antiquity; and so long as the Family is
an enduring social fact and the unit of civilization,

this conception will never be discredited. But there have been many times during Christian history when it has not been very potent.

To claim that the Christian centuries witness no change in the thought of God, is absurd. Obviously, the disciple of Boniface in the eighth century Northern forests, had not the same image in mind as the modern worshipper. A monarchical and judicial conception ruled the feudal period, when King and Judge represented ultimate power, and theoretically at least ultimate justice: all mediæval art instinctively pictures Deity under one or another of these forms. Theistic abstractions, seeking with dubious success to realize a Great First Cause, emerge during the eighteenth century. When the People began, in the revolutionary age, to come to their own and to develop class consciousness, visible emblems of a Divine authority faded, as we have seen, replaced by burning intuition of a Universal Presence. This intuition has deepened during the gradual rise of democracy; yet within its scope may be discerned varying stress, corresponding to minor phases of social experience. For instance, the intense domesticity of the Victorian period in England saw devout souls like F. D. Maurice reviving with passionate devotion the tender conception of the Divine Fatherhood; the

Lord of Battles has been invoked of late with atavistic ardor by nations delivered over to a militaristic ideal.

And through all these tentative and conditioned gropings may dimly be discerned the Eternal and the Abiding. He Who is "Himself unmoved, all motion's source," is truly seen in every age, but seen in different aspects, as a mountain remains firm yet presents a new vision to each new angle of approach.

Facing this vast diversity, what excuse can be found for asserting any one ancient formula to be final? Why in any case cling to a formula defined, not by Christ Himself or His immediate followers, but some centuries after His death?

"The right faith is," says the Athanasian creed with sublime serenity: and again, "This is the Catholic faith: which except a man believe faithfully, he can not be saved." Can the arrogant dogmatism encounter anything but ridicule?

The challenge is fair; but the Christian answer is simple. No one defends any longer the Athanasian attitude toward the unbeliever; but the Christian is none the less quite sure that the symbol of the Trinity, as found in that glorious Athanasian Hymn of Praise, is the noblest expression of man's best and richest religious thought which has ever yet been evolved. He easily perceives that the doctrine is not explicitly found in the words of Christ or even of Paul; but he has only to read the passages appointed for Epistle and Gospel on Trinity Sunday to perceive also that it is an inevitable inference from the Scriptures.

His faith, however, is based far more deeply than on Scriptural authority alone. The more he examines the Trinitarian formula, in its seemingly preposterous paradox, the more he discerns that it comprehends marvellously all elements which have been vital at any stage of race-experience. His conviction grows that no fruitful thinking on Divine Mysteries has yet escaped the confines of Trinitarian faith, however unconscious men have been of the relation, and he is inclined to think that all new speculation, so far as it is based on experience of spiritual reality, will continue to be provided for within these confines. The Christian loyal to Catholic tradition has no difficulty in believing that the constant prayer of the Church has been answered, and that the Spirit has taught her the true Hallowing of the Name.

To demonstrate this bold statement would take another book than this. Only a few hints, humbly proffered, can be given here.

It has just been noticed how constantly the

double craving for Unity and for Multiplicity has marked religious and philosophical speculation. Plain monotheism satisfies scientific minds less and less; it will be recalled that William James was so well aware of this fact that he recommended Polytheism as the more rational religion! Yet ordinary polytheism, with a number of separate and independent deities reclining on Olympus or intervening often at cross-purposes in human affairs, is not likely to revive.

The interdependence and unity of life become more striking from the revelations of every laboratory. Our own being, if we look within, is multiplex, though the whirl of concentric personalities apparently, under conditions of health, focusses in one centre. Here is a mystery into which at our present stage of knowledge it is dangerous for most of us to peer; but psychology, no less than metaphysics and science, drives us to recognize that Unity is not so simple a matter as naïf speculation assumes. Many, yet one,—oneness in manyness,—only this paradox can express the truth of personality human or divine.

Again: the hope of the ages has clung, now to an Infinite Purity untouched by the imperfections of this universe, abiding in primal light and calm and joy: now to a human God, subject to mortal struggle, divine in virtue of suffering, limitation, and growth; now to an all-pervading Spirit, slowly coming to its own through the dross of matter. None of these conceptions can be sacrificed. Cautious philosophers may bid us fling the Absolute on the scrap heap of ideological waste; but plain people will never rest without it: theologians of some types bid us discard a limited God; but plain people insist that only with this kind of God can they take comfort and find fellowship. However the infinite distance of the Creator from His creation may be stressed, plain people know themselves to share an undivided life, and feel this life sweep in plastic stress throughout the universe. All these ideas must be synthesized in an idea of Deity which can offer a man something to pray to, no matter by what path his pilgrim feet follow the eternal quest.

Can any one suggest a better means of satisfying the very real, pragmatic needs of brain and heart than that afforded by the ancient doctrine? These are not recondite reflections fit for a theological seminary; they are the obvious thoughts of a simple Christian, as he sings his Holy, Holy, Holy, recites his Apostles' Creed, or receives the benediction of the grace of Christ, the love of God, the fellowship of the Spirit. The doctrine of the Trinity is like all doctrines, tentative and symbolic; but it is the most practical doctrine ever formulated. It does not attempt to solve any mystery, it states nothing about the how, the method, of the union of manyness in oneness. It simply corresponds to experience. It summarizes and fuses the aspirations of the ages; each new discovery of our nature or the nature of physical life corroborates it. And the race has not grown up to it yet.

For, if Trinitarian thought is the best reflection of religious experience in the past, it as surely points to the future; and only in that future can it thoroughly come to its own.

The doctrine of the Trinity has been the chief force which has slowly instilled democracy into the world. This assertion will seem grotesque and fantastic enough to the outsider; but the Christian should see the truth of it at once.

In the first place, the great reality which the doctrine presses home is that Love is in its nature eternal and absolute. This assurance the Theist, whether Unitarian or Jew, must, it would seem, hold with more hesitancy, except by an assumption which saves his faith at the expense of his reason. Sentiment aside, nature and history bear quite inadequate witness to a God of Love, however inexorably they suggest a God of Law. To enable us to believe in ''L'Amor che muove il sole

e l'altre stelle," revelation must supplement ob-
servation. And revelation, short of the full Catholic conception, is incomplete. Monotheism at
best contemplates a self-existent and self-sufficing
Deity, who in the dark backward and abysm of
Time was moved to create a universe: and the
reflection arises that in the eternity which underlies time and precedes it, He must have been either
a very cold Deity or a very pathetic one. Love, to
such thinking, is accident rather than substance in
the Divine Nature; or at least, if one tries to think
of the Creator at all apart from His creation, one
perceives within His Being the quality, rather
than the activity, of love. But the love on which
we lean must be more than this. It must be at
the source of things, primal, creative, from all
eternity. God *is* Love.

Love, as we know from our own hampered experience, implies interaction among diverse centres of consciousness. According to formal logic,
such centres are incompatible with unity: according to our most intimate contact with life, they
are necessary to it: for real Oneness can never
be realized in isolation. That is quite as great a
paradox on the human plane as on the divine. We
realize the fullness of our own being only when
we are conjoined in love to other beings, and gain
our best hints of unity and completeness of life in

sacred flashes when hearts and minds, retaining their separateness, through their very separation realize the mystery and miracle of fusion. Such flashes are rare and fugitive; it is possible that many people are never visited by them. But they are real, they do happen; and a suggestion is in them of the Divine interweavings wherein the full richness of Infinitude must abide.

Three Persons in One God! The phrase is an obsolete scholastic absurdity to shallow moderns; yet no other symbol could so well express the report of human experience as to the only sort of Oneness which can be substantial and complete. The practical, satisfying, quality of the doctrine has been discerned by Christian experience all down the ages. Richard of S. Victor [1] worked the matter out with exquisite insight in a passage found in English form in the fourteenth century *Mirror* of St. Edmund:—

"Dere frend, thou art to wit there is but One Godde. And thou art to wit that no good may fail in Godde; but bycause that swete thing and good thing is comfort of fellawschippe therefore may not Godde be withoute goodnesse of fellawschippe. Then behooveth it that there were many persons in Godde the Heyest Goodnesse. . . . And bycause

[1] De Trinitate, III, 2, III, 11. Cited in E. Gardner's translation. The Book of St. Bernard on the Love of God, p. 169.

that Onehead is good and Manyhead also, therefore it behooved that Onehead and Manyhead both
were in Godde. And by this skill comes man to
the knowing of Godde, that He is a Godde in Himself and Three in Persons." [1]

And here is a modern Bishop:—

"The uncaused self-existent Eternal is indeed,
One, One God. But within the bright shrine
and sanctuary of Godhead, there is more-than-
oneness. Deity is no bright solitude, but the Scene
of mutual affection. Deity contains forever the
mighty flow and movement of an infinite Life of
responding interacting Love." [2]

But among non-inspired writers, Dante regards
the Mystery with most enlightened as with most
profound adoration: —

"O grace abounding whereby I presumed to fix
my look on the eternal light, so long that I consumed my sight therein! Within its depths I saw
ingathered, bound by Love in one volume, the
scattered leaves of all the universe. O Light
Eternal, Who only in Thyself abidest, only Thyself dost understand, and to Thyself self-under-
stood, self-understanding, turnest love and smil-
ing!" [3]

[1] Richard Rolle of Hampole. Ed. C. Horstmans. Swan Sonnenschein, 1895. I, 238 (slightly modernized).
[2] Bishop Monte: Quoted in The Sacred Lessons. Duttons,
p. 197.
[3] Paradiso, XXXIII.

Such reflections on the eternal outgoings of Love which faith discerns in the heart of Deity are well summed up in the succinct, pregnant phrase of Phillips Brooks: "That social thought of God which we call the doctrine of the Trinity." As another modern thinker has said, the Christian ideal is not a divine Person but a divine Society.

not a singularity but a holy Trinity — loving Comm-unity

So far, we have been dwelling on the partial truth that man makes God in his own image. But, for faith, there is a deeper meaning in the reciprocal truth and in the opposite sequence. We Christians believe that as man is forever seeking to know God, so God is forever seeking to reveal Himself to man: and the successive conceptions of Deity all represent a meeting-point of human strivings (colored as they must be by temporal conditions), and of Divine manifestation. For us, moreover, the Divine Power has triumphed in the work of the Spirit of Pentecost, through whom a revelation of the Divine Nature has been given, as perfect and permanent as our poor mortality can apprehend. "Howbeit when He, the Spirit of Truth is come, He shall guide you into all the truth: for He shall not speak from Himself; but whatsoever He shall hear, these shall He speak. . . . He shall glorify Me; for He shall take of Mine and shall declare it unto you. All things

whatsoever the Father hath are Mine.'' We dare
to believe that the promise is fulfilled, and that,
in Holy Writ and in the Mind of the Church, can
be found not merely the record of our own desires,
but shining glimpses of Reality.

''Let Us make Man in Our image,'' says the
mystical account of the Creation. However schol-
arship may account for the strange plural by the
dim polytheistic suggestion in the Elohim term,
the Christian mind sees here at lowest the assumption that the idea of God is the norm by
which human society must be shaped, the type to
which it must ultimately conform.

Perhaps for some of the reasons already given,
Trinities have satisfied groping devotion in many
an ancient religion. Nevertheless, it would seem
hardly short of a miracle that such an idea as the
Christian Trinity should have been formulated
in the fourth century, and a continued miracle
that throughout the period of imperialist or feudal
autocracy, the Church should have cherished a
conception to which so little in the life of Society
or the State could be said to correspond.

In such divergence of the concept of God from
anything which could have emanated from below,
the Church finds evidence of the Divine Impress
on her mind, or, to use a rather discredited word,
of inspiration. The doctrine was pregnant with

prophetic meanings; but it is only today, as democracy comes to its own, that these meanings can be fully perceived. The time has come to attain the consummate adoration of the Triune God by shaping our human relationships in His Likeness.

What was Athanasius doing when he fought his great fight for the Homoousion? Nothing more important than this: he was defending the truth yet unborn that social harmony depends not on differentiation of rank but on diversity of function. The great Creed associated with the name of the saint is a magnificent manifesto of faith in social equality: "The glory equal, the majesty co-eternal. . . . And in this Trinity none is afore or after other; none is greater or less than another, but the whole three Persons are co-eternal together and co-equal so that in all things as is aforesaid, the Unity in Trinity and Trinity in Unity is to be worshipped."

Wise and glorious words. For in truth, that perpetual interchange of love which is the life of the Divine Unity, is possible only between equals. There is a love which stoops, there is a love which adores; but the ultimate and primal love is no mere impulse of Creator toward created. It is no dependence of inferior on superior. It flows from heart to heart, in one circle forever renewed. And the Catholic doctrine of the Ever-Blessed Trinity results from no scholastic split-ting of hairs but from the true though in-adequately expressed intuition of the highest type of social life. Christian thinking, in the stage on which it is just beginning to enter, discovers amazed in the ancient doctrine the conception of the Nature of Deity best adapted to inspire social progress and to be the soul of the new world toward which we move.

The task of the ages is to evolve a society which shall subsist in a unity of love that shall bear some likeness to the Divine Nature in Whose Image we are made. But this task must be slowly fulfilled. It could not be fairly envisaged, even, until the evil of social inequalities was clearly perceived, and the face of man was turned toward the Cooperative Commonwealth. During feudal times, the necessity for inequality as the basis of civilization was never questioned by practical men. Christian philosophers like Marsiglio of Padua and Wyclif, to be sure, developed daring communistic ideas.[1] But the common run of

[1] It is interesting to note that in the Spiritual Franciscans from whom these men derive, social radicalism is associated with immanential and pantheistic heresies: another witness that emphasis on the work of the Spirit leads to democratic and egalitarian ideas.

maybe the current political & social chaos is leading us to this awareness.

mediæval thought, ignoring the latent implications of theology, conceived God as a great Autocrat, from Whom authority descended in grades, by a system supposed to ensure social stability in accord with divine law.

It was a noble system in its day; but it broke up. Coincident, broadly speaking, with the decay of feudalism and the birth of democracy, came a new sense of the Divine Immanence; modern civilization has realized in a measure that dispensation of the Spirit which completes the dispensation of the Father and the Son. Religious intuition and social institutions altered together; a people adoring the Blessed Trinity could never, in the long run, hold to a monarchical society of graded ranks; and by the reverse truth, no monarchical conception could satisfy a socialized world. In the ultimate Christian vision, as in the social faith of the free nations, there is no room for aristocratic principles or for confidence in an autocracy.

Thus the doctrine of the Holy Trinity has down the ages borne firm unrecognized witness to democracy; and as the democratic leaven works, the time ripens for full understanding of the social implications of Christian thought. While Deity was thought of as separate from His world, the doctrine might well seem unreal and obsolete. But the Threefold Name becomes the heavenly prototype of earthly society, as soon as we recognize God to be the Spirit within as well as the Father and the Redeemer; and our Christian duty is plainly seen to be the release and reproduction of the Divine Nature in the corporate life of the race. For the final relation of man to his God is not submission or subjection, but re-creation.

As Christian men learn this high concept of their duty, they will receive plain guidance in political and social energies. The doctrine of the Trinity furnishes the norm of the relationships we must establish and the functions we must perform; it is the Image of the only society in which we dare to rest. The Church, if she will rise to the height of her great argument, can reveal democracy to itself in all its spiritual glory. She steadfastly holds up to adoration a unity of interacting Powers, wherein is no higher nor lower but functions varying and ranks coordinate, and in so doing, she presents a truth far ahead of what the State has realized. She discredits forever to Christian logic the fallacy that real progress can be secured and valid incentives obtained by competition and inequality. The Creative Life of God is the model and example for man; only a society of equals can reflect the perfect energies of perfect love; and as the Church gains self-knowledge, she must range herself with the most advanced egalitarian tendencies. When she so obstinately rejected the early heresies which tried to establish distinctions within the Divine Glory, she was unconsciously furnishing a standard by which all political and social movements must be judged. She was preparing the way for that social ideal which has at last entered the arena of practical politics, and is struggling for victory in every civilized land. Should that ideal triumph, the Church has nothing to fear. She will find herself in harmony as never before with Society and with the State.

Surely the American divine, Alexander V. G. Allen, was right when he spoke in ringing words of "that ancient Catholic charter of human freedom, the doctrine of the Trinity."

This diversity of function which faith discerns in the Infinite and Eternal Energy,—what is it? Here too we can find help for the shaping of our mortal life. The Church forever adores the Creative Force which is perpetual Fatherhood, the redemptive Force through which ravaged creation is restored, the sanctifying Force by which it is sustained. This is the eternal Outgoing from the Eternal Life, in threefold guise. And humanity should conform in all its varying activities to one or another phase of this flux of life within the Godhead. Creating, redeeming, sanctifying,—this is our human business. Energies which can not come under one of these heads are at least open to suspicion; and a society in which these three energies proceed in healthful harmony, will possess all conceivable richness of life.

Creative power in humanity shows itself of course only in a secondary and derivative way. Yet to look at a wheat-field is to realize that it is given us to cooperate with life,—enhancing, directing, releasing. Cities, bridges, the shaping touch of the teacher on the mind of the taught,—"the flash of the Will that Can," not only in music, but in every form of art,—all these attest our immediate share in creative power.

But since we live, as Deity must also live, in a world fallen and perverted, we are privileged to be one not only with creating, but also with redeeming love. What vast human activities are thus united, thence inspired! Philanthropy, medical work, all direct spiritual activity aiming at the conversion of sinners, every energy of restoration and renewal, reflect the redemptive phase of the Divine Nature. It is the unprecedented development of these energies which has given Christian civilization its distinctive character; as is natural in a religion which is especially and characteristically the Faith of the Cross.

And as we may in our measure create, and in union with Christ restore, so by virtue of the Spirit within us, it is granted us to sustain. All energies which go to the inspiration and continuance of institutions, or to the maintaining of personal life: all forward looking adventures which seek the progressive release of the divine life through the human, are one with the work of the Holy Spirit of God.

As men choose their place according to their respective aptitudes in these multiform and glorious types of activity, they help the Divine self-expression. Creation, restoration, maintenance,—they are the great social functions, derived, as Catholic faith discerns, from the very Name of the Most High.

To compare this Name with the world we know is to be filled with dismay. There are abundant uses for our energy outside the scope suggested. There is energy which destroys rather than creates, which poisons rather than restores, which congeals rather than releases the springs of life. Of late years, such energy has seemed to dominate the world, while the works of consolation, relief and reconstruction, vast in themselves, have dwindled to nothing in comparison. Moreover,

even in times of peace and prosperity, civilization
is in no sense a mirror of the life of God. For
those distinctions of rank, wealth, privilege, to
which we blindly cling, have no prototype in the
Catholic thought of the Divine Nature.

These things are the Enemy. They are the
shadow cast upon our mortal plane from that
Dark Power forever opposed to the Father of
Lights. The Christian Church is here to fight
them with her might; and whatever our dismay,
we have no reason for despair. Social intuition,
outside the Churches, is growing up to the great
intuitions of Christianity; and as soon as Christians understand better what is implied in their
own doctrines, and join forces with all activity,
from whatever source, which presses toward the
purpose of their Lord, a new day will dawn. They
will see without possibility of question, where to
align themselves in the welter of modern thought;
and they will devote themselves wholly and only
to such activities as find sanction in the Activity
of God. They will be centrally concerned with
the progressive hallowing of the Holy Name,
through the reproduction of the Divine Nature and
the Divine Energies in the social order. In proportion as they so shape and limit their lives, they
will build on earth the New Jerusalem: the Ideal

Commonwealth which needs no temple because illumined by the fire of sacrificial love.

On Trinity Sunday, the Church calls us to join in the worship of all creation, perpetual behind the veil of sense. Humanity and the lower orders of being are united with the Godhead in perfect harmony; the mystic Beasts are drawn within the very arcana; for they are "in the midst of the throne" as well as around it; and, full of eyes within, dowered with inward sight, they join with humanity at its wisest, in singing for ever the Holy, Holy, Holy of a world redeemed. Theirs is the consummation of desire, the Vision, before, behind, within, of Very Love. "Every thing that lives, is holy," said William Blake, in a dangerous paradox of supreme audacity; perhaps he had shared the vision of those in the midst of the Throne, who see eternal Reality. For Trinity leads us through the shows of things into the sanctuary of abiding truth; and for a moment, as we keep the Feast, we children of process escape our finitude. There is a burning peace to Trinity Tide:

"Hitherto we have celebrated His great works; henceforth we magnify Himself. Now, for twenty-five weeks we represent in figure what is to be hereafter. We enter into our rest, by entering in with Him Who, having wrought and suffered, has opened the Kingdom of Heaven to all believers. For half a year we stand still, as if occupied solely in adoring Him, and with the Seraphim in the text crying, 'Holy, Holy, Holy' continually. . . After Christmas, Easter and Whitsuntide come Trinity Sunday and the weeks that follow; and in like manner, after our soul's anxious travail; after the birth of the Spirit; after trial and temptation; after sorrow and pain; after daily dyings to the world; after daily risings unto holiness; at length comes that 'rest which remaineth' unto the people of God. "[1]

"Occupied solely in adoring Him": yes; and the best adoration is the fulfilment of simplest duty. The study of practical ethics, to which the last half of the Christian Year is devoted, is carried on in the tranquillity of full understanding and of attained vision. Having summoned us to give our thanks and to sing our Trisagion with the mystic Fellowship of the Redeemed, and with all visible creation, Mother Church has taught us all she knows. Very serenely, very ardently, we are henceforth to learn under her guidance to apply that knowledge. None the less, her Mys-

[1] John Henry Newman: "Parochial and Plain Sermons," p. 369. Rivingtons, 1869.

teries are never fathomed, never exhausted; lessons learned must be forever learned once more, and the truths she teaches flash a new light in each generation. In due time, patiently and eagerly, she will call us to begin the great Sequence once again.

CHAPTER X: THE EUCHARIST

Antiphon: I am the Living Bread which came down from Heaven: if any man eat of this Bread, he shall live forever. Alleluia.

V. Come unto Me, all ye that travail and are heavy laden,

R. And I will refresh you.

We offer and present unto Thee, O Lord, ourselves, our souls and bodies, to be a reasonable, holy, and living sacrifice unto Thee; humbly beseeching Thee, that we, and all others who shall be partakers of this Holy Communion, may worthily receive the most precious Body and Blood of Thy Son Jesus Christ, be filled with Thy grace and heavenly benediction, and made one body with Him, that He may dwell in us and we in Him.   Amen.

CHAPTER X: THE EUCHARIST

THE rhythm on which the beauty of language depends results from a continuous interweaving of constants and variables; and the deeper beauty of either speech or song springs from the subtlety of the interweaving. Nor is this law true of language only. The call of rhythm is one of the deepest to which men respond, and all loveliness, whether of the Spring or of the stars, obeys it. That hidden rhythm which is the pulse of the Breath of God through all things, creates the harmony of the world; and as the insight of philosophy grows more profound, as the insight of science grows keener, they discern and reveal more clearly the immutable permanence of proportion and relation which underlies all the seeming chaos and confusion of form in the visible universe. The old Greeks were sound in their intuitions:—

"In all God's works,—(as Plato cries
He doth),—He should geometrize."

What is true of Nature is true of all noble art;

and nothing responds more perfectly than the great art of Catholic worship, to this mystery of rhythm, with its changes and modulations depend-ent on an unchanging base. In the Church Year, the colors on the Altar from Advent violet to the scarlet of Christmas and Whitsuntide, the white of Easter, the green of Trinity, are vestments for the varying passion of the soul: and the sequence of Christian experience, following the Footsteps of Christ from Bethlehem to Calvary, meets our innate need for movement, purpose, quest. But the other need of permanence is also met; it is on the One Altar that the changing colors glow, and the successive phases of Christian emotion all rest there like homing birds; finding their centre and their goal before the Perpetual Sacrifice, in adoration of the Lamb slain from the foundation of the world.

Week by week the varying Collects, Epistles and Gospels which we have studied with such lov-ing care, are preludes to the unaltered Canon of the Eucharist,—the most ancient as it is the most enduring portion of the Liturgy. Now and again, on the chief festal days,—Christmas, Easter, Ascension, Whitsunday and Trinity,—the feeling of the season penetrates the very sanctuary, and imparts special intention to the ever-repeated

Sanctus of which neither angels nor men can weary. But the Eucharistic worship as a whole does not alter. It is the fundamental factor in the eternal rhythm; it supplies in the Catholic and supernatural life what the imperfectly discerned realities of mathematical proportion supply to the growth and movement of the visible world.

Here at the Altar, devotion sees the centre and focus of all the truths taught by successive seasons. Here these truths are suddenly and gloriously revealed as no mere commemoration of past history, but as living and eternal fact. We "show forth the Lord's death till He come," and so reiterate the Advent hope, recalling the promise in the Upper Chamber that He will eat with us the fruit of the Vine, new, in the Kingdom of His Father. The Eucharist is Bethlehem made perpetual, a continual Incarnation, as Old Masters knew well when they filled the Manger of the Babe with a bed of ripe wheat ears. Redemption is consummated in the endless sacrifice of Him Who is both Priest and Victim; yet the Food of Immortality preserves body and soul unto everlasting life in the eternal Easter. The Word and Holy Spirit forever consecrate these elements, that they may renew within us the Sevenfold

Gift. And here supremely at the Altar the faithful chant their Sanctus, Sanctus, Sanctus, adoring the Blessed Trinity Who unites them with Himself through their union with the Sacred Humanity of God sacrificed for men.

It is on Holy Thursday that the historic sense of the Church naturally bids us remember the Institution of the Lord's Supper. The Roman Communion, always enlarging on the implications of primitive faith, sets apart in August her Corpus Christi Day, that when "the fields are white to harvest" men may see

> "As in a glass, the timeless mystery
> Of love whereby we feed
> On God, our Bread indeed." [1]

Yet a special Festival is hardly needed, since week by week the Eucharistic Feast, inexhaustible centre of mystic experience, incandescent with the love of God, welcomes the faithful to the vision of Eternal Truth behind the Sacramental Veil.

What are the social emphases in this crowning Feast, wherein our triumph and our sorrow meet, and the personal life of the soul finds its most sacred expression?

[1] Evelyn Underhill: Corpus Christi.

If we examine the Office of Holy Communion in the Prayer-Book, we shall find that even in a superficial way these emphases are not neglected. They are particularly clear in the introductory portion, preceding the ancient Anaphora or Canon of the Mass which opens with the Sursum Corda. The refreshingly explicit moral sense of the Reformation has put its impress on all this part of the Service. The initiate who would draw near to the central Christian Mysteries is not prepared, as in Oriental cults, by isolation from his fellows. No self-mortification nor psychical disciplines are proposed to him. He is rather bidden, again and again, to be sure he is in right relations to his fellow-men. The "minister" in the introductory rubric is stoutly told to forbid the Sacrament to any one "known to have done any wrong to his neighbors by word or deed," thereby offending the congregation; the same order is to be used with those betwixt whom he perceives malice and hatred to reign. The good old custom has lapsed in the modern Church, and suggestions are not lacking that its revival might make for reality and social health. But perhaps it is wise to be content with the later admonition to those who would approach the Altar, that they "amend their lives, and be in perfect charity with all men"; and again that they be "in love and charity with their neighbors, and intend to lead a new life": a searching command, surely, if applied, for instance, to the class struggle.

At all events, one of the most striking and characteristic liturgical achievements of the Reformation was the insertion of the Ten Commandments, interweaving them with the old Kyrie Eleison, at the outset of the Communion Office. The practice obtains today of substituting the positive beauty of Our Lord's summary of the Law,—in which all social duty is implicit,—for the harsh and negative Hebrew form; but it is certainly well that the Law, in one form or another, should sturdily guard the entrance to the most mystical of rites. And perhaps it would do us no harm, as in penitence and shame we face the modern world, to repeat the Ten Commandments a little oftener. Murder, stealing, impurity, and covetousness are not obsolete; we might profitably remember how long ago the race gained moral insight enough to disapprove of them; the rehearsal of the ancient prohibitions is an excellent prelude to the Heavenly Feast.

A Collect for obedience; the special Collects, Epistle, and Gospel, which give to the day its distinctive color; the great Confession of Faith,— in use in the West in this connection since the

seventh century. Then come the Alms, an inter-
ruption to the sentimentalist, and probably a
rather perfunctory form to most people. Yet
they were part of the Lord's own Service from
primitive times. The Christian attitude toward
property is not to be ignored as we approach the
Altar; and the appointed Sentences are saturate
with it. Notice that it is not enough, according
to two of these sentences, "to do good," or to be
"ready to give," we must be also "glad to distribute," a far more radical precept, especially
if one looks up the word distribute in the Greek.

The great Intercession for the Church Militant
is a safeguard against all private-mindedness in
the quest of union with God, Church and State
and all God's people. The suffering, the sick and
the perplexed and the faithful departed,—these
are present in our hearts as we draw near to take
the Body of the Lord. Confession, absolution,
and the preparation is complete. It has carried
with it severe reminders of social duty; and now
the faithful are ready to hear the strengthening
Words, to lift up their hearts and to sing their
Sanctus with all the company of Heaven.

From this point, it is no longer the time for
consciousness of social duty. "Solus cum Solo,"
man enters the Sanctuary where surrender and
aspiration meet, and where satisfaction awaits the

immemorial hunger of the soul. Yet no sooner has he returned from the Altar than the old thought is renewed. The great corporate prayer of Christ Himself for the Coming of the Kingdom and the Doing of the Will on earth is the first that may be uttered by lips which have received the Holy Mysteries; part of the Eucharistic joy is the knowledge that we are very members incorporate in that Mystical Body which is the blessed company of all faithful people; and the Gloria in Excelsis recalls the Peace to men of good will to which the heart forever clings.

Thus all the careful worship through which the Church leads her children to the Altar, all the emotion into which, cleansed and fed, they return, is saturate with social earnestness. But the Sacrament is greater than the worship which enshrines it; and meditation on the Holy Mystery Itself gives best guidance to our minds.

The simple and outstanding fact is plain; this is the Sacrament of Unity, this is the Feast of Brotherhood, this is the sure communion no less of man with man than of man with God. It is to the Christian the earnest and the pledge of that Holy Fellowship and Perpetual Feast in the Kingdom of Heaven where all separateness shall be done away. Alas, that down through history the

Sacrament of Unity has so often been a Sacrament of division; alas that still we rear our separate Altars, and defy brotherhood where we should most and first assert it. None the less, despite the perplexities and blunders of Christ's stupid though loving folk, the great Rite stands forever as witness to the abiding truth of fellowship. The Holiest Gift is not given to us in solitude; Christian wisdom forbids a solitary approach to the Altar. Only at the common meal, where two or three are gathered together, do we touch Infinity most intimately, and find ourselves most fully one with Creative Love.

The Eucharist, rightly understood, destroys all barriers. We being many, are One Bread, One Body. "As the elements of the Holy Bread, scattered in the mountains, were brought together into a single whole, may Thy sanctified Church be gathered together from the four winds of Heaven, from the ends of the earth, out of every nation and country and city and village and house, into the kingdom which Thou hast prepared for it." This ancient prayer of the second or third century shows Christianity more potent than the Pax Romana to inspire ideals of unity in a divided world. Here, in Love's home, class, rank, race, nation, vanish; opinions cease to separate as men unite in the Act prescribed by the common Lord.

Theories about the Sacrament may vex the mind of Christendom; but no Christian carries them to the Altar. The sacramental life, as it quickens at the touch of faith, is the same in every heart. The Eucharist is the final rebuke to the instinct for spiritual aristocracy. Saint, ascetic, administrator, theologian, priest, has no higher privilege than the least of repentant sinners. No esoteric grace, conditioned on wisdom or even on spiritual attainment, awaits the Christian initiate. All is open to the child just confirmed, to the most ignorant of loving hearts; at the first cry of faith, the Gift is ready. It unites us with the whole Church militant here below; and no less, with the Church expectant and triumphant.

> "Angels and living saints and dead
> But one communion make,"

in the democracy of the Altar.

The associations of the Feast are the most homely and most universal, and the social message lies on the surface, even for those to whom the Communion means a memorial service and nothing more. What is it we remember? A group of friends gathered around a table, eating ordinary food; men troubled, perplexed, but quieted by the loving talk of their Leader, and drawn by

the power of His words into deep assurance of
their oneness with Him and with God. The
historic situation is implicit in our memory of that
Paschal meal. The solemn commemoration of the
deliverance of a nation from bondage; the anxious
consciousness of danger and defeat shared by all
members of the little group, aware even while
they scrupulously observe the highest traditions
of their race, that they are outlawed in the opinion
of their national authorities. Their feeling
toward their Master and toward one another has
the intensity which always obtains among people
standing against a hostile world for an unpopular cause, and, as usually happens in such
groups, the doubter is present, and the traitor.
Nevertheless, above their haunting fears, their
petty rivalries and suspicions, penetrating their
stupidity and their imperfect apprehension of the
very ideal which unites them, sounds the Voice of
Love. It bids them remember Him in the daily
breaking of their bread, and the very simplicity
of the command is quiet proof that the ideal for
which Love faces death shall never perish in
their hearts.

The Master leaves His faithful no illusion as
to what awaits them. The world is going to hate
them as it is hating Him, and they are not to be
surprised at the fact. But joy such as the world

does not know, joy which no man can take from them, will also be their portion: the supreme joy of knowing themselves branches of the fruit-bearing Vine. Here is the Eucharist indeed.

Christian experience rejoices in these holy memories; but it has not stopped with them. Inevitably and insensibly it has penetrated deeper into the essential meaning of the rite which it observes in remembrance of its Lord. The Eucharist is more than a memorial, it is a sacrament: the most abiding contacts of man with eternity are centred here as in their home. The Gift of Christ to his own is perpetual reality, and past, present and future meet at the Altar in an eternal Now. It was like Jesus to make the commonest of food, prepared by man from the dawn of history, the instrument of the greatest mystery. The Eucharistic Feast beautifully sanctifies the union of the life of Nature with human labor. Wild roots and berries are not the chosen means of communicating Divine Life, but rather the wheat and the grape which men have grown. So the final benediction descends on our dressing and keeping the garden of the world, and in reward of our tender care, the fruits of the earth become the Food of Immortality. Here is the consummation of all toil, the healthful, sacramental consecration whereby the temporal is linked with the eternal, and physical life with life beyond the cognizance of sense. Beyond and around every Altar, the imaginative eye sees fields all over the earth billowing with grain, vineyards covering the hills; and it sees that the myriad men who bend to the work whereby the world is fed are all unconsciously nourishing the soul as well as the body of the race in a sacramental harmony.

There is something mysterious in the emotion which seizes any sensitive person in presence of the older types of agricultural labor. Sowing, reaping, threshing, ploughing,—the sight of them touches the springs of tears; no other call is deep as theirs in the normal life of man. Is this because all labor is implicit in the fundamental labor of tilling the earth? Or is the feeling rooted in some intuition of a mystic sanctity inherent in the feeding of men? In the Eucharist, such sanctity receives its ultimate seal, "Give us this day our daily, our superstantial bread": the devout heart has always gathered double meaning into the petition. It desires to unite physical nourishment with the nourishment which sustains the body and the soul alike unto everlasting life.

But the harmony is broken. The wheat is ground, the grapes are crushed. They have yielded up their natural life that they may min-

ister to human need, and until they have thus suffered they can not be transformed into the Body
of the Lord, given for our salvation. This holy
Sacrament is a continued Incarnation, ever revealing the Word made Flesh; it is also the
eternal sacrifice, wherein Love dies that we may
live. The sternest spiritual law finds here its
best, most solemn and complete expression; man
feeds upon his God.

Here we approach an aspect of the Eucharist
seldom touched on except by the enemies of a
sacramental system. But it is an aspect which
can not rightly be ignored, and it is charged with
social significance. The ancient Office, so dear
to us from the associations of long Christian centuries, leads the faithful back to the simple glory
of the scene in the Upper Chamber, where friends
conscious of impending disaster entered into a
new pact of unconquerable loyalty and love. But
in certain suggestions, the rite antedates Christianity altogether. As far back as we can gaze,
man has known the strange instinct of sacrifice;
and the human beings sometimes offered in the
twilight of his early history may have been representatives or substitutes for a divinity. Crude
beliefs and shocking rituals bequeath their echoes
to the exalted worship of the Christian mystery.

Most plain Christians are probably ignorant of

these associations or turn their minds away. But they do ill; for it is the supreme triumph of our holy faith to abandon nothing which has been sacred to man, to justify and include every intuition, every aspiration, by which he has sought to claim his heritage in the supernatural world. A wise instinct made Gregory the Great bid the anxious Augustine not to rebuke but to assimilate the heathen practises dear to the old inhabitants of England; in the same way, a wise instinct rejoices today in the discoveries, more and more numerous, often flaunted in our face by the opponents of Christianity, of the extent to which our religion has absorbed Pagan rites and primitive superstitions. All these dim, strange outreachings of the spirit to the Eternal, these embryonic efforts to penetrate the awful mystery of existence, had in them a spark of vital fire, a germ of the growing soul: all find in Christianity the fulfilment of their groping need:—

"Types and shadows have their ending,
For the newer rite is here,"

The noble liturgical words of the Eucharistic hymn apply, not only to the Jewish sacrifices which were the direct precursors of the Christian Sacrament, but also to many other strange faiths and customs which seem at first a dark and obsolete chapter in the soul's long story.

By how many myriads of ancient men has the earth been conceived as the Body of the Nourishing God! Still, in Italy, grains grown in darkness through Lent are placed, during the holy days when the Passion is commemorated, around the image of the dead Christ; as in Egypt, how many centuries ago, wheat ears were sculptured, springing from the body of Osiris. Awful and repellant rites, in which the worshipper drank the blood of the victim that it might instil into his body an immortal power, were current through the Roman Empire when Christianity was young, and in these rites our own faith is shadowed. These ancient cults, these wild imaginings, all held to something that we cannot abandon today; they centred in the recognition that life must be given for the support of life: life both above us and beneath us in the scale of being; wheat and grape, becoming by transmutation the Body and Blood of the sacrificed God. The Eucharist accepts this recognition to the full. It preserves the past of humanity in all the pathos of its aspiration; it is the victorious transfiguration of what seems darkest and wildest in primitive religion, of what is felt to be most humiliating in practical experience, into the ultimate expression of the law of sacrificial love.

Willingness to accept the death of God offered that we may live, to take the ever-renewed sacrifice into that ever-changing being which can otherwise not live at all, is the ultimate act of faith. It is the seal on the awful mystery of interdependence, the lie forever to all attempt to live a self-sufficing life. Existence itself is a continual Communion, in which man feeds upon the universal God.

How can this tragic necessity be turned into a Eucharist? Only by man's becoming one with his God, and in that oneness offering himself for the life of the world. In the deep mystery of union with the Passion is the redemption of the lowest necessity of our being, and its transformation into the highest glory. How gladly, how solemnly, must he who nourishes himself by the perpetual dying of God offer himself, his soul and body, to be a reasonable holy and living sacrifice, whereby humanity shall be fed! We kneel at the Altar, less to receive a gift than to be united with the Giver, and the surrender which is the law of Christian life finds here its abiding source of strength. Dying to live, we attain our true being:

"Crushed and tormented in the mills of God,
And offered at life's hands, a living Eucharist."[1]

[1] Evelyn Underhill, Corpus Christi.

Offered forever, as we are forever sustained.

Every humblest Christian tests this paradox every day. Calvary precedes Easter, and Christ's folk must give themselves with their Master if they would receive His salvation. The paradox becomes a platitude when written down; but it is daily translated, thank God, into lovely realities of character. It strikes the basic note which distinguishes the Christian ideal from every other. The strict disciplines, the noble self-control, demanded by the Greeks, for instance, were to the end of perfecting the individual; the Christian pursues these virtues with the salvation of others rather than his personal perfection, as his goal. His being is suffused with a consciousness of the Whole life, human and divine, which he shares through the ceaseless activity of giving and receiving. He lives, silently, in an order in which the laws of self-seeking are superseded by the law of the Broken Body and the Shed Blood. It is a law which can only be obeyed by union with the sacrifice of God.

And when this life is really lived, human nature is generally acknowledged, even by people of hostile sympathies, to reach its highest point. Let no one dare to talk as if Christianity were a failure; he shall be bidden lift his eyes to the countless, mainly uncanonized, saints, who shine like stars in the all-embracing sky. Christianity has been a triumphant success because the Christian type of personality is the fairest achievement of the ages. In the full Christian life, the truths of atonement and resurrection are raised from passively recognized principles into experienced fact, and even remote observers perceive their glory. Men and women attain the most exquisite beauty of their possible being when they yield themselves to the Sacramental Law.

Alas! this law of personal life has never, since the time of Christ, been accepted as the law of social life also; yet it is enshrined at the heart of a Sacrament which is the communion of the Whole Body of the Lord. Nations, classes, disregard it as completely as if Christ had never been born; but it is the only law of their redemption, or even of their continued existence. No civilization founded on self-defense and self-assertion can ever endure. It can have only a phantasmal and transitory life; for it belongs to the lower order of decay and death, not to the enduring Sacramental order, where the natural carries within it the seed of immortality. There is not one ethic for individuals, another for the State. The corporate and the personal life, if they would enjoy the same heritage of permanence, must follow the same law; here again, as so often before, we find that the Christian ethic, which has proved life-giving to the individual, must be socialized if the Will of the Master is to be fulfilled.

But corporate obedience may well seem impossible to the natural man; for this is a law above Nature. The Christian, more than any one else perhaps, must doubt whether the tremendous changes involved in the establishment of a new world-order can be wrought on the natural level.

Desperate attempts on this level are witnessed today, and the good and evil in them is strangely confused. More than one modern mystic believes that the socialist movement has a suggestion of Antichrist; and so far as this movement repudiates religion and ignores God, it may well terrify spiritual men. In their distrust they are joined by nearly all types of the fleshly mind. The historian shrugs his shoulders, the psychologist shakes his head, the man on the street breaks into contemptuous laughter. They know, all these, that only a minority ever responds to the higher law; they see how imperfectly it works even in the saints; they observe that we shall always have human nature to reckon with, and they never fail to reiterate with an air of finality that you must alter human nature before a cooperative society would work. From the point of view of the world, they have a strong case.

But what has the Christian to do with the point of view of the world? Let him be careful as to the allies he chooses in this crisis, lest he make the Great Refusal.

The Christian does not dare to be a pessimist. He is the optimist of the ages. He knows, because he sees it happen, that human nature is being altered day by day, hour by hour, through the inflowing power of the Grace of God. The whole teaching of his holy faith, as revealed throughout the Christian Year, is that a supernatural force, limited only by our unbelief, is released into this mortal world. The Eucharist preserves bodies as well as souls unto everlasting life; it bears perpetual witness that the economic and political life of earth is to be the Sacramental expression of Immortal Love. We who accept the dying of God as the source of our continued life, can never despair when love seems denied and destroyed in the movement of the world-drama. We know full well that it dies to live, and to draw those who in ignorance violate it, into unity with its holy life and its redemptive power.

The logical votary of a Sacramental philosophy will never reject the theories and movements which press toward a more fraternal world, on the score that such schemes are too visionary, and transcend the possibilities of humanity. Rather, he will hasten to put at their service the spiritual dynamic which he commands. Christianity is not the acceptance of a creed but the entrance into a life, and in that sacramental life timid distrust of high possibilities has no place. The recreation of society in the Divine Likeness is possible, but possible only in the strength of the regenerate life, born from Above. In proportion as men open their being to that inflowing life, given to them in Baptism, sustained at the Altar, they will prove competent to sustain a social order founded on sacrificial love.

To alter human nature is the task explicitly entrusted to the Church of Christ. Unless in the present crisis she bends herself to this task with a wider vision, in a supreme Act of Faith in her own Sacraments, she will crucify the Son of God afresh. This is the hour toward which she has been moving since her birth at Pentecost. She has outgrown asceticism and otherworldliness, with their subtly atheistic denial of the Incarnation; she is ready to understand her own ideals as never before. The mighty forces at work for the overthrow of the aristocratic order and the establishment of social democracy, will either wreck or save the civilized world. The choice between these alternatives rests with Christians, and with the Church which feeds them with the Bread of Life.

The solution for which the weary world has waited long is in the midst of us. Let us not forget at this moment that *now* are we the sons of God. In every nation of the West goes on the stormy process of preparing a new economic body for the race to use. It can be the privilege of Christianity to turn that process into a Sacrament by infusing into it the soul it needs. The Adventure is great and full of hope, for the Christian spirit is more pervasive than we think. It works among multitudes who do not consciously profess the Name of Christ, but who live in a civilization suffused for nigh two thousand years by Christian ideas. Among those others who retain a definite creed and membership in some Christian communion, it waits, in ignorance and bewilderment often, but in exceeding great desire. It needs to become incarnate, and the time for this incarnation is at hand. Every Eucharist brings to the Christian radical the courage and the strength he needs; for as he receives the Gift of the Body and the Blood, he knows that he is made one with the Divine Humanity which, lifted up in sacrifice, draws all men unto Him, and which forever speaks out of the eternal glory the revolutionary and re-creative words, "Behold, I make all things new."

Made in the USA
Middletown, DE
24 August 2018